"Tim Smith hits the nail on the head! ɪɪ⌐ , ˲ . Paul said that we're to raise our children 'in the training and instruction of the Lord.' That's raising disciples, not just nice kids! Sound tough? This book maps it out and makes it easy!"

RICK OSBORNE, *author of* Amazing and Unexplainable Things in the Bible *and other books for boys*

"If you're looking for a parenting resource that will make you feel all warm and fuzzy, put this book down. But if you truly want your kids to grow up with the kind of godly character that will help them be people of integrity and strength, then start reading. Tim's words will challenge you and make you rethink your assumptions about what it means to be a parent. This book will not only change your ideas, it will change your family."

CARLA BARNHILL, *author of* The Myth of the Perfect Mother

"Tim Smith said it so well: 'Strong parents produce strong kids. Weak parents produce weak kids.' In the pages of this book, Tim will guide and encourage you to be 'strong parents.' Step up to the plate and the enjoy the responsibility and the privilege of being a parent."

KENDRA SMILEY, *coauthor of* Be the Parent

"Tim Smith is one of America's finest and most refreshing parenting experts. This book will show you how to raise your kids to be responsible adults. It is a fresh approach and very practical."

JIM BURNS, *President of HomeWord and author of* The 10 Building Blocks for a Healthy, Happy Family

"A fantastic book for parenting the next generation. Great insights. The best I've read!"

BILL MYERS, *author of* The Incredible Worlds of Wally McDoogle *children's series*

"Tim Smith shows parents why pulling the weeds of bad behavior isn't enough. We must also nurture the roots of a good heart. This book is filled with practical ways to fill our homes with grace and love, so our children will be able to face the world they live in."

OLIVIA BRUNER, *author of* PlayStation Nation: Protect Your Child from Video Game Addiction

"While reading this book, I was reminded of Jesus' question: 'What good will it be to gain the whole world and yet forfeit our souls?' As parents, it is so tempting to focus on our children's academic achievements, athletic awards, good looks and future career success. In the process, we often neglect opportunities to influence and shape their Christian character. Tim Smith challenges us to move beyond raising nice, wimpy children. We cannot afford to just give our children what they want or what we want them to have. Instead, to live as Christians our children are going to need traits such as courage, discernment, compassion, empathy and contentment. This book provides parents with practical steps to help our children develop these important qualities."

DENNIS LOWE, *Psychologist and Director of the Center for the Family at Pepperdine University*

The Danger of Raising

NICE KIDS

PREPARING OUR CHILDREN
TO CHANGE THEIR WORLD

Timothy Smith

IVP Books

An imprint of InterVarsity Press
Downers Grove, Illinois

InterVarsity Press
P.O. Box 1400, Downers Grove, IL 60515-1426
World Wide Web: www.ivpress.com
E-mail: email@ivpress.com

InterVarsity Press® is the book-publishing division of InterVarsity Christian Fellowship/USA®, a student movement active on campus at hundreds of universities, colleges and schools of nursing in the United States of America, and a member movement of the International Fellowship of Evangelical Students. For information about local and regional activities, write Public Relations Dept., InterVarsity Christian Fellowship/USA, 6400 Schroeder Rd., P.O. Box 7895, Madison, WI 53707-7895, or visit the IVCF website at <www.intervarsity.org>.

Scripture quotations marked NIV are taken from the Holy Bible, New International Version®. NIV®. Copyright ©1973, 1978, 1984 by International Bible Society. Used by permission of Zondervan Publishing House. All rights reserved.

Scripture quotations marked NLT are taken from the Holy Bible, New Living Translation, copyright ©1996. Used by permission of Tyndale House Publishers, Inc., Wheaton, Illinois 60189. All rights reserved.

Scripture quotations marked "The Message" are from The Message. Copyright © 1993, 1994, 1995. Used by permission of NavPress Publishing Group. All rights reserved.

Published in association with the literary agency of WordServe Literary Group, Ltd., 10152 Knoll Circle, Highlands Ranch, CO, 80129.

All stories are true. The names and some details have been changed to protect privacy.

Design: Cindy Kiple
Images: Image 100/Getty Images

ISBN-10: 0-8308-3375-7
ISBN-13: 978-0-8308-3375-7

Printed in the United States of America ∞

Library of Congress Cataloging-in-Publication Data

Smith, Tim, 1954-
   The danger of raising nice kids: preparing our children to change
   their world/Timothy Smith.
     p. cm.
   Includes bibliographical references.
   ISBN-13: 978-0-8308-3375-7 (pbk.: alk. paper)
   ISBN-10: 0-8308-3375-7 (pbk.: alk. paper)
   1. Christian education—Home training. 2. Christian education of
   children. 3. Child rearing—Religious aspects—Christianity. 4.
   Parenting—Religious aspects—Christianity. I. Title
   BV1590.S58 2006
   248.8'45—dc22

                                      2006003975

P	20	19	18	17	16	15	14	13	12	11	10	9	8	7	6	5	4	3
Y	22	21	20	19	18	17	16	15	14	13	12	11	10	09	08	07		

Contents

Foreword

When it comes to raising kids that are ready to take on the future, there's an easy mistake that we can make that undermines our plans. It's the mistake of working overtime to raise nice kids. I see it all the time. It's like a fatal flaw in so many of the parents I work with. And when you focus in on one of the most conscientious groups of parents out there—moms and dads who claim a strong faith in God—it's pandemic.

Let's make sure we don't confuse *nice* with *good*. They are not synonyms. *Nice* more often equates with the word *safe*. Safe kids tend to develop their moral character in a comfortable environment, an environment that limits the risks that a child must process. The scenario I've just mentioned is a classic recipe for mediocrity.

The goal of effective parenting is not to raise safe, nice kids. It's to raise strong ones. Living a purposeful and influential life requires taking risk—lots and lots of calculated daily risks. But the risks can be processed within the context of a well-guarded harbor. That's what our homes can represent to our children. The fact is, home is where life is making up its mind. Therefore our homes must provide the kind of framework that encourages children to make some of the most dangerous decisions of their life. It's where they need to decide what their mission in life is going to be, who their mate is going to be and, most important, who their master is going to be.

Here's the problem. Our fears get in our way. We see the toxic competition that culture often throws at our kids, we sense their fragile inner core, and we calculate our own sense of inadequacy as parents, and the next thing you know we're doing everything we can to bring our children up in surroundings that offer as little threat to their values and convictions as possible. Unfortunately, this strategy lends itself to an anemic faith, listless individuality and an anchorless value system.

You can raise kids prepared to stand on their own two feet without having to throw them to the wolves of our culture—especially when they are young and ill equipped to handle the pressure. The guidebook to see you through is in your hands. Tim Smith has a street-level understanding of what it takes to raise kids fit for active duty as adults. He's been training parents for decades. His words are steeped in experience and saturated with grace. He's winsome and kind even as he retrofits us for a better way of seeing our job as parents. *The Danger of Raising Nice Kids* will give you a ton of help while saving you a lot of heartache.

There's a reason someone made up the saying "Nice guys finish last." The last thing you want to have happen is to raise kids that are easily influenced, intimidated, defenseless, culturally defined, unprepared and irrelevant to the world they take on once they are out on their own. I invite you to pick up the cadence with one of America's great family coaches and learn better ways to raise kids who are ready for tomorrow. Nice kids? No. Strong, emotionally fit and morally good? Absolutely. You're going to enjoy *The Danger of Raising Nice Kids*.

Dr. Tim Kimmel
Author of *Raising Kids for True Greatness*

1

More Than *Nice*

We don't need another parenting book that promises *nice* kids. There are too many out there already—I wrote a few of them myself. Being nice just doesn't cut it anymore, not in the new millennium. In case you didn't notice, things have changed. You might point to fanatical terrorism, the new millennium, the rise of the hip-hop culture or retro fashions. Whatever you want to point to as the cause, things are different. And a parenting philosophy that focuses only on external behavior is destined to fail.

What do I mean by *nice*? A pleasant, friendly, well-mannered, carefully groomed, preferably conservatively dressed person. Isn't that what we want our kids to be?

My trusty Webster's dictionary says that at one point *nice* meant "strange, lazy, foolish," coming from a Latin root for "ignorant," literally "not knowing." I don't want my child to be a nice ignorant fool, too lazy to accomplish anything! So in these pages, I will be challenging the practice of *parenting from the outside,* focusing on a child's looks, behavior and performance. How do we nurture kids who aren't ignorant? who aren't foolish? who aren't naive?

NICE BRIAN

"Dude, I hear it was crankin' at Zeroes. Wanna go there?" asked Brian on our way to go surfing.

"Sure," I said, "You're not gonna wimp out if it's double overhead?"

"Me? I'm not a wuss. Bring it on!" He thumped his hand on the passenger door of my SUV to the beat of U2 on the CD player. At fifteen, he was a hot surfer with the looks of a teen fashion model and a bevy of beauties as his entourage.

Once a week I went surfing with some of the high school students from our church youth group. On this day southern California was in the midst of a warm August, and a huge south swell was rolling in from Mexico.

"Is it really going to be ten foot?" asked Tom, a novice surfer, also fifteen.

"That's what the website said. Six to eight at Zuma, so you know it will be bigger at Zeroes. It catches everything!"

"I might just watch from the beach," Tom confessed.

"Wuss!" Brian punched his arm.

"Oww—hey Brian, aren't you grounded?"

I turned and looked at Brian, raising an eyebrow.

"Don't give me that look, dude. It's cool with my folks. They let me go today, but I have to stay home tonight."

"Why? What happened, Brian?"

He shot a mean look at Tom. "Well, I got busted. I was at a party last weekend, and we ran out of beer."

Brian was Tom's friend and was new to the youth group. He was courteous and respectful to adults, got decent grades, was very popular and wore the hippest clothes. He did better at choosing fashion than at choosing friends. Except for Tom, most of his friends were partiers.

"So what did you do?"

He flashed his perfect, ultra-white smile. "I set 'em up."

"How can you do that? You're fifteen and don't drive."

Brian laughed. "It wasn't dark yet, so I got on my bike and rode to 7-11. When Sahib wasn't watching, I snagged a twelve-pack."

"You ripped off a twelve-pack of beer? On your bike?"

"Yeah." He looked down at the carpet. "But the dude saw me and called the cops—who happened to be next door at the donut shop!"

"You're kidding!"

"Nah, it's true. So I tried to outrun him. He turned on his lights and siren. I was screaming through the neighborhood; but he was gaining on me, so I tossed the beer in the ditch. I rode faster without the weight, but the cop was getting ticked. He yelled through the microphone, 'Pull over! You are under arrest!' But I ignored him and kept pedaling. He swerved his cruiser onto the sidewalk in front of me and knocked me off the bike. I tried to run, but he caught me, handcuffed me and threw me in the back of his car. He recovered the beer as evidence and hauled me to jail."

"Did you have to stay long?" I asked.

"Nah, it was actually a holding cell for juveniles. I was the only one there. My parents signed me out two hours later."

"So now you are grounded?"

"Yup, this is my first outing all week. It's cuz I told my pops that Timmy and Tommy are good influences on me that he went for it."

Brian looked like he had it all together—engaging personality, popularity, girls, looks, clothes, money, brains, skill in sports, comfort with adults. You would say that Brian was a nice teenager.

But on the inside Brian was void of any real substance or self-confidence. His biggest fear was that his friends would reject him, that he would be labeled "uncool." His worst nightmare became a reality when the cruiser lights came on.

If you had run into Brian on his way into 7-11, he would have held the door for you and you would have thought, *What a courteous and handsome young man.* And you would have been right. He was polite, good-looking and suave with adults. In a word, he was nice.

Being nice is not enough.

THE DIVERSION OF NICENESS

One danger of raising nice kids is that they will end up too delicate. Kids who can't make it in the real world. Kids who may look good on the outside but lack internal strength and courage. Kids who give in to peer and cultural pressure.

A lot of what passes as advice to parents, including advice to Christian parents, will help us raise nice kids. Nice *wimpy* kids. Kids without backbone, passion or courage. In this era, kids like that will be destroyed.

Our kids need to be more than nice.

I'm not saying I want kids not to be nice. Our kids need to be *more than* nice.

We live in a culture that is not child friendly. It is increasingly becoming antifamily. It is already antimarriage. We need to prepare bold combatants to challenge such hostile surroundings. Why?

Because children are important to us. Family is important to us. Marriage is important to us.

So this isn't just another parenting book. This is a guide to take you to the next level of parenting, where you actually disciple your child. It will show you how to go far beyond influencing your children's behavior to influence their heart, mind and skills for life.

You will discover how to grow a child with passion. You will learn how to capture your child's heart and ignite her God-given passion.

You will find out how to develop and strengthen your child's convictions. You will learn to parent with purpose, to grow integrity within yourself and your child.

You will discern how to develop nine critical qualities that most parents fail to develop in their children. Qualities that will help them survive and prevail in the challenging times in which they are coming of age. Qualities that will help them become warriors, not wusses.

Here are the nine forgotten qualities that most parents don't teach:

- vision

- authenticity

- listening

- empathy

- compassion

- discernment

- boundaries

- contentment

- passionate love

Why don't parents teach these? Because they don't know how. Because their parents didn't teach them. Because they don't have time. Because they are in survival mode, dealing with behavior issues, with no time to think through purposeful parenting. Because they have focused on the externals and not given much thought to preparing the heart of their child. Because they don't know how to model values and teach skills.

Don't worry, this discusion doesn't have to get weird. It doesn't have to be that hard either. In fact, I'll try to make it fun along the way. And I promise to keep it practical.

Theologian Henri Nouwen wrote of a time he was working with

some other monks on a new church building, side by side with the construction crew. The construction workers were used to swearing, and they kept at it even though men of the cloth were around.

After several days of their cursing and taking the Lord's name in vain, Henri exploded. "Don't you know you are not supposed to curse!"

Tension filled the site. Everyone became angry. Understanding disappeared in the wind. The next day back on the job the swearing picked up again. A few raucous outbursts of taking Jesus' name in vain came from one particular bricklayer.

Many parents don't know how to model values and teach skills.

A monk named Anthony quietly approached and put his arm around him. "Hey, you know—this is a monastery—and we love that man here."

The man looked up from his work, smiled, "To tell ya the truth—so do I."

They both laughed. And after that simple exchange, everything changed.[1]

That is my aim with *The Danger of Raising Nice Kids*. Let's change things. We don't have to force them. It doesn't have to be political. We don't have to be stressed over the culture wars. Sometimes the best way to influence people is with a hug and a laugh.

I'm surprised I survived my reckless childhood. I walked a mile to school in the snow (unsupervised), wandered away for hours at a time, rode my bike miles away from home, chatted with strangers at the bus depot, spent several nights in a tree house in a vacant lot, and figured out how to make bombs out of firecrackers—all of this before I turned ten!

If you had asked my mom what I was up to or where I was, she would have responded, "He's out playing somewhere. I'm sure he'll be home before it gets dark." Then she would have returned to the tasks of raising four children. By today's standards my mother would be negligent, and the neighbors would call Children's Protective Services.

But my mother was not negligent. She was representative of the moms of that time and place. Even though she didn't cart us kids in a minivan to a plethora of activities—soccer, art lessons, tutoring, karate, scouts, music lessons, Bible club—I rarely remember being bored, and we didn't even have PlayStation!

I don't think my mom ever heard the saying "Every moment is a teachable moment." I don't think she was too concerned with our "enrichment." I assume she was more concerned with survival. In some ways growing up then was more natural: kids were what they were. What you see is what you get. This was before the high priests of psychology and child development admonished us to "nurture" children and give them every advantage for enrichment in an increasingly competitive world. This was before prenatal brain-stimulus classes in response to parents' desire to raise their baby's IQ.

"This is the most protected generation ever," said a church's children's director, a former elementary school teacher. I had traveled to her church in rural Indiana to present a parenting seminar. The town had fewer than eight thousand people. Most homes were built on two-acre or larger plots. The horizon was dotted with silos and barns. It looked pretty safe to me.

"Parents don't let their kids play in the yard unless they watch them. Most of the time they don't let them. They just pack them in the van and take them to organized lessons and sports, then they watch them."

The most protected generation ever. The phrase continued to ring in my head. *What could be dangerous out here—a couple of cows charging your yard?* Coming from Los Angeles, I couldn't relate. But if parents don't feel that their kids are safe in rural Indiana, they probably don't feel that they are safe anywhere.

I think many parents in our culture are driven by fear. Fear that something bad will happen to their kids. Fear that they will not give their kids the right blend of enrichment experiences. Fear that they will raise kids with weak self-esteem.

I hear about these fears when I meet parents at my seminars, and I deal with them in my family coaching practice, where I work with parents and with teens like Chelsea.

TROPHY CHILD

Seventeen-year-old Chelsea, one of my clients, told me, "My mom is paranoid about not being the perfect mom. She always pumps me up like she's my cheerleader. She always says, 'great job' even though I know I choked. I know it's fake. I know she means well, but it's empty."

"There's a difference between empty praise and genuine words of affirmation," I said.

"Exactly. She wants me to feel so good about myself that it isn't realistic. I don't always do well, but she pretends that I do."

"Yeah, the whole self-esteem campaign pushes praise, even if it's exaggerated, so that you will be happy, feel good about yourself and not use drugs."

Chelsea smiled, "I know, I'm a DARE graduate. But feeling good about yourself doesn't come from the outside; it's more from the inside, and it needs to be based on reality."

"Right. You want to feel worthwhile, competent and capable, but it needs to be based on real stuff, not just the old 'super job!' line."

"Yeah, my mom is like Ben Stiller's parents in *Meet the Fockers*. When Bernie Focker proudly displays his grown son's awards to the in-laws, Robert DeNiro's character responds, 'I didn't know they made ninth-place ribbons.' And Bernie says, 'They have them up to tenth place,' then gestures toward all of the awards prominently showcased on the Gaylord Focker wall of fame. 'There's a bunch on the "A for Effort" shelf there.'"

We laughed.

"False praise creates fragile people. We want people to feel good about themselves for the right reasons, Chelsea. We don't want them to feel they've accomplished something when they really haven't. As a result of this esteem obsession, we have a generation who thinks they are entitled to things without working for them."

"Yeah, I've seen that with my sister's friends. They think they will graduate from college, get a high-paying job and get promoted six months later. They think they are going to start at the lifestyle level where their parents are and move up from there. They are devastated when they have to move back home and work in retail."

"Not the right time to say 'Great job,' is it?"

OBSESSION WITH PERFECTION

Our culture is obsessed with perfection: perfect babies, intelligent preschoolers, kindergartners who speak French, third-graders who know algebra, fifth-graders who make the all-star club team in soccer, eighth-graders who spend their Saturday's in SAT prep courses.

Moms have been told, "You can have it all; you can handle work and the demands of a family. You just need balance." *Newsweek* magazine reports that this obsession is having an impact:

> The idea that *that's enough* is a tough sell in our current culture.
> We live in a perfection society now, in which it is possible to
> make our bodies last longer, to manipulate our faces so the lines
> of laughter and distress are wiped out. We believe in the illusion

of control, and nowhere has that become more powerful—and more pernicious—than in the phenomenon of manic mother-hood.[2]

The Perfect Mommy is one expression of manic motherhood: the drive to be the postfeminist woman who is highly educated and com-petitive at work *and* the nurturing, responsive mother who has her kids in all the "right" activities and still maintains her figure. Some-times the challenge can become overwhelming. Sixty-five percent of women with school-age children feel stressed and don't feel like they have enough time.[3]

Judith Warner articulates the pressures in her article "Mommy Madness":

> LIFE HAPPENED. WE BECAME MOTHERS. And found, when we set out to "balance" our lives—and in particular to balance some semblance of the girls and women we had been against the mothers we'd become—that there was no way to make this most basic of "balancing acts" work. Life was hard. It was stress-ful. It was expensive. Jobs—and children—were demanding. And the ambitious form of motherhood most of us wanted to practice was utterly incompatible with any kind of outside work, or friendship, or life, generally.[4]

For many moms, and dads too, life is much harder than they an-ticipated. They really did believe that with the right education they'd get the right job, and with the right job they'd reach a level of income and status that would bring fulfillment. In some cases these expecta-tions did come true, but a majority of parents struggle hard to fit it all in, and most wonder if they are really able to pull it off. They set the alarm clock a half-hour earlier, make lists and buy a bigger calendar to squeeze in all of the family activities, thinking, *Someday I'll be able to slow down and take care of myself.*

JEN'S SURPRISE

"We were concerned about the public schools, and we wanted to give our children the best education. So we home-schooled our oldest, Jen, and she responded very well to the individualized attention," explained a woman who had attended my parenting seminar. "I wish I had heard your presentation five years ago."

"Why, what happened?" I asked.

"We liked the idea of going through the curriculum at your own pace, and Jen's was fast. She liked to get her work done by noon so she'd have the rest of the day free. We let her get a job when she was fourteen; she graduated at fifteen and started working full time and going to community college at night. We didn't realize that we had raised a pathological liar. It turns out she used her intelligence to manipulate and deceive us. She had this whole other life . . ." The mother's voice trailed off. I could tell she was on the verge of tears.

"She excelled at academics but failed at life?"

"Exactly." She dabbed her eyes and looked up. "We thought she was a good Christian girl, and wow, could she talk the talk, but her heart wasn't in it. She was living a lie, and we were too naive to catch it.

"I liked what you said today about perfectionist parents. We were focused on her grades, how she looked, her attitude and how her performance made us look good, like she's some kind of prodigy, this product of our home. It turns out she met a married man at work, had an affair with him for two years and got pregnant. He divorced his wife and left his two kids for Jen. Last Saturday they got married. I tried to get the pastor of his church to see the damage, but he performed the ceremony anyway. She's eight months pregnant, married to an older man, and she's only nineteen years old!"

She grew up too fast, I thought. Jen's freedom and responsibility didn't match her moral development. She had an adult life without the structure of adult character.

Hurrying children through childhood usually produces disastrous results. Jen's situation reminded me of one of my favorite quotes from David Elkind:

> People under stress tend to see other people in the shorthand of symbols. Because they are under stress, not only are they self-centered, they also lack energy for dealing with issues apart from themselves. Symbols, oversimplifications really, are energy-conserving. Parents under stress see their children as symbols because it is the least demanding way to deal with them. A student, a skater, a tennis player, a confidant are clear-cut symbols, easy guides for what to think, to see, and how to behave. Symbols thus free the parent from the energy-consuming task of knowing the child as a totality, a whole person.[5]

Jen's mom had settled for a symbol instead of knowing and raising her real daughter. Jen was a status symbol to her parents: the Bright Home-Schooled Progeny. It made them all feel good, but it didn't prepare Jen for life.

When we are hurried or under stress, we tend to hurry our children through childhood. Hurried children, like Jen, work more than they play, and they too become stressed.

We need to resist our culture and allow our children to grow up slowly. We need to protect their innocence and allow them to develop wholly—physically, emotionally, mentally, morally and spiritually. When we hurry children, natural development is not possible in all these areas. And, as in Jen's case, the results can be disastrous.

Don't be afraid of your child. Don't be afraid to draw the line. Children need a solid moral center—an anchor that provides stability while they choose friends, discern the right decisions and perceive others with empathy. Be willing to challenge the parenting trends that have produced hurried, disconnected families and uncommunicative kids with an insatiable sense of entitlement and a disregard for rules. Consider medical doctor Robert Shaw's words:

When we are hurried or under stress, we tend to hurry our children through childhood.

> This epidemic seeps like a fog into all of our culture. Parents find themselves enslaved by a materialistic, overarching society that leads them to spend so many hours at work and so much money that they can't make the time to do the things necessary to bond with their children. They are worried that they might crush their children, stifle their self-esteem, or kill their creativity, to the extent that they lose all sense of proportion about the role of a young child in a family. They rarely put limits on their children or permit them to experience frustration, and they overlook their children's moral and spiritual development.[6]

I'm not calling for a return to the 1950s postwar idealism—because behind this nostalgia lays discrimination, prejudice, hysteria, and a lack of rights and opportunities, especially for women and ethnic minorities. No, I don't want to go back. I want to go forward.

We need to come to terms with how we see ourselves. Growing up with a "can-do" orientation fostered by pop psychology, we saw our-selves as winners. We were bred for competition. We wanted to beat the Russians to the moon. We wanted to beat the Japanese in the world economy. We wanted to beat everyone at the Olympics. We be-lieved that we could ascend to our highest aspirations and that we would mature into the capable, successful, hip adults we always dreamed we could be.

We pass on our competitive nature to our kids. We strive to give our children every advantage. We want our daughters to excel at sci-ence and math and show the boys they can. We want our sons to "reach their full potential" in all areas and still be in touch with their feminine side. We see ourselves as winners. In a way, it's a redux of social Darwinism—only the strong survive. In order to be fit and sur-vive, we need to have advantages over the weak.

What would happen if, instead of seeing ourselves as winners, we began to look at ourselves as trainers? What if, instead of focusing on the competitive edge of parenting, we focused on questions like these: How can I train my child? How can I prepare her for life? How can I develop his character? How do I grow and train a child from the inside out?

Raising kids in this millennium requires more than giving them self-esteem or a competitive edge. We need to train them to take crit-icism without falling apart. We need to permit scenarios in which they fail but learn that failure is never final, unless you blame some-one else. Some of the greatest life lessons can be learned from our fail-ures, if we are willing. We need to help our children develop accurate views of themselves, with a clear-cut analysis of their strengths and weaknesses, instead of a hyped-up self-esteem based on shallow slo-gans. We want them to feel good about themselves without thinking *god* of themselves.

PERFECT TEETH

We make sure our children have perfect teeth. We scrape to save for the orthodontist or refinance the house to pay for braces. It's expensive and requires dozens of visits over a period of years, but the result is the perfect smile.

I submit that the perfect smile is the icon for today's child. I'm not against orthodontists or good dental care, just proposing perfect teeth as a symbol of all our efforts as parents. He's not born with it, but through effort, expense and sacrifice, he's gonna have the perfect smile. It's costly, demands time, is repetitive and uncomfortable, and our kids complain about it, but the end result is a gleaming, symmetrical smile, worthy of a magazine cover.

We are raising a generation with perfect teeth and twisted hearts. Because of our investment, they have nice teeth, but their hearts are warped. They haven't learned compassion, empathy and initiative. They haven't developed personal convictions and moral standards. They feel okay about themselves because they have been told that they are "good," but deep down inside they wonder, *Am I really good? Do I have what it takes to make it? Does life require more of me than being nice?*

In a culture that opposes many biblical commitments, being nice will not equip our children to be effective. Being nice will not help them advance the kingdom of God with their convictions, behavior and influence. Being nice won't help them stand apart.

Instead of socializing our children into the predominant norms of our society, we need to strategically train them to engage and challenge these norms and views. We need to model for them the values that we hold dear, and we need to teach them qualities and skills that will make a difference in their lives and in the lives of others. In a word, we need to *disciple* our children.

2

Parenting
as Discipleship

I facilitate a men's breakfast group on Tuesdays. Our group is called Family Man, and we are learning about life's most important relationships—those with our wife and our kids. We start the day with coffee and basic stuff like "Treat your wife better than your car," "Your kids are not your employees," and "You can still be a man and ask for directions."

One morning, one of the guys in my group said, "My friend lets his son have a TV in his room. Recently, he bought him a laptop, and he has wifi so the kid can cruise the Web. This weekend his son had a friend over who is a few years older. When the dad went to check on them, he found them perusing porn sites. The kid's only nine years old! What should he do?"

Sometimes our kids can throw us a curve as we try to raise them with moral guidelines. As Christian parents, we want to pass on lasting values to our kids. To do this, we need a perspective that is transcultural and not simply a product of our culture. We need a long-term perspective that is not obsessed with short-term payoffs. We need a biblical model, based on principles that outlast the trendy voices of our current culture.

Biblical parenting is more than modifying our children's behavior. It's much deeper than that. It's more than raising compliant, well-mannered kids to be nice.

As Christian parents, we are not to simply socialize our children into civil human beings; we are to train them to advance the kingdom of God. Christian parenting is less like a cotillion and more like boot camp. It's not simply about manners and proper decorum in public; it's about being conditioned and prepared to take on life's challenges. It's not about fussing with their collar so they'll look cute at the dance. It's about getting them ready to do battle.

Biblical parenting is more than modifying our children's behavior.

Tim Stafford highlights some of the demands involved:

We live in an era when traditional beliefs have been tossed aside and when popular culture—television, movies and music—displays terribly corrosive morality. Families are much shakier than they used to be. You can no longer assume—if you ever could—that solid values will be passed on from one generation to the next. Building families takes careful, intentional work.[1]

We aren't sending our kids to a dance; we are sending them into a cosmic contest. Are you preparing yours?

FLEX TIME

As our children mature, our style of parenting has to flex, particularly when it comes to making them mind. We need to progress from a punishment orientation to a discipline orientation. When our children are young, we use punishment to train them. We may spank

them, send them to their room, give them a timeout or turn off the
TV. Punishment is a penalty imposed to correct misbehavior.

Punishment may be appropriate for controlling and directing preschoolers. But as our children get older, we do well to move from
punishment to discipline. Discipline introduces the ideas of personal
responsibility and choices through consequences as a means of training. Natural consequences happen in the natural course of events.
But often the costs of allowing natural consequences would be too
high. We would be crazy to say, "If you ride your skateboard on the
busy street, don't come limpin' to me when you get hit!" Further,
sometimes natural consequences are not immediate.

Instead of letting our kids learn from natural consequences, we
can introduce *logical consequences*—consequences we set up in advance with our child, aiming to help her make wise choices and
know what results her choice will bring.

Punishment doesn't always teach our kids. It requires a moral
judgment by the parent: "You made a mess. Go to your room!" Consequences help the child learn moral responsibility: "You made a
mess. Clean it up."

Punishment tends to focus on the past and on behavior. Discipline
tends to focus on the present and on our child's will.

Most parenting books stop here, content to show parents how to
stop the misbehavior, fix the strong-willed child or help the child
take personal responsibility for his choices. These are all helpful
skills for parents. But let's not stop there. We are on a mission from
God. We have been called by him to raise up the next generation of
moral leaders. We need to move beyond punishment and discipline
to discipleship.

That's right, we are to disciple our kids, just as Christ discipled his
followers.

Have you ever thought of parenting as discipleship? I didn't say "discipline," I said discipleship. Don't worry—you don't have to wear baggy cotton tunics and leather sandals (unless you want to!). You don't have to trade in the minivan for a pair of donkeys. Discipleship isn't just for the first-century Christians of the Middle East. Discipleship is for high-tech urban and suburban families (and rural ones too) who have never seen a camel.

We need to move beyond punishment and discipline to discipleship.

Discipleship is an intimate, personal relationship designed for growth and learning through imitation, dialogue and observation. The English words *disciple* and *discipline* stem from a common Latin root, *discipulus,* or "learner." Discipling is learning through an intimate, personal relationship.

Discipline should be understood not as punishment but as teaching of self-discipline, an internalization of values through a relationship. This kind of teaching is done by example, not by coercion or force. If we are to understand parenting as discipleship, the primary goal of parenting isn't teaching, it's modeling.

Thinking in terms of punishment leads us to focus on behavioral control and stopping what our child is doing. Parents who see their role as discipleship, however, will focus more on what their child is learning in relationship to them, especially in circumstances that we would consider disciplinary.

Noted psychologist Bruno Bettelheim explains:

> The idea of discipleship implies not just the learning of specific skills and facts, but acquiring these from a master in whose image one wishes to form oneself because one admires this indi-

vidual's work and life. This usually involves sustained, close personal contact, one personality being formed under the impact of the other.[2]

Parenting, like discipleship, is a teaching/learning relationship. Our kids are learning from us whether we intend to be teaching them or not. Children *are* the disciples of their parents, for better or worse. Parents teach by word or example, through every interaction they have with their children.

Seeing parenting as discipleship helps us get a broader view of our role. Parents who only use punishment or discipline to solve an immediate problem may be teaching their children the wrong lesson. That is, "Change your behavior and I'll leave you alone."

The primary goal of parenting isn't teaching, it's modeling.

The motive of discipline is to get a child to obey. But compliance isn't enough in a culture that will chew up and destroy teens and young adults who are not mature. Discipleship focuses on the mentoring relationship between parent and child. It focuses on what the child learns, not simply changing his or her behavior. The motive of discipleship is to nurture the child toward maturity.

Discipleship is a close relationship that provides a personal example for the child. It concentrates on maturing the child from the inside out.

A focus on discipline generally creates compliant kids, but it rarely produces courageous ones. Now, I am not advocating a permissive style of parenting; I am calling us to a more demanding style of parenting—one that requires us to change and grow and provide the example. Discipleship calls on us to set the pace, knowing that our children are most likely to absorb the values they see lived out in our lives. We can teach them skills, but we need to show, not tell, when it comes to what we say is important. Consider the contrasts between discipline and discipleship, laid out in table 1.

Table 1. Discipline Versus Discipleship

Discipline	Discipleship
Goal: Nice kids	Goal: Mature influencers
Punish, correct	Model and pass on self-control
Control behavior	Promote growth and learning
Focus: Child's behavior	Focus: Child's learning and preparation
External	Internal
Personality	Character
Maintain peace in the family	Integrate personal virtues
Force and control	Relationship and influence
Power	Authority
Instruction	Modeling
Reflection for the child	Reflection and dialogue for the child and parent
Battle	Tutorial
Primarily extrinsic motivation	Intrinsic and extrinsic motivation
Compliance (submit to the standard)	Cooperative (allows for individual differences)
Now (immediate)	Process (allow for change over time)
Action	Attitude
Submission	Mentoring
Behavior and thinking	Feeling, thinking, deciding and behaving
Child changes behavior	Child and parent mature

External-focused parenting produces kids who look nice on the outside. If our emphasis as parents has been on the outside, then we should expect to have kids with an external focus. They will have learned from us how to act. They will have picked up from us that *doing* is more important than *being*.

Note that discipleship means that *both* the child and the parent mature. It's not about just the growth and behavior of the child. Discipleship considers the moral and spiritual development of every family member, beginning with the parent.

If a child, particularly a teenager, sees his parent growing and working on the same issues she is trying to develop in him, he will be more open to the values transfer and less likely to rebel. Why? Because *growth is something we do as a family.* Growth does not simply mean "changing the kids' behavior."

Some of the most difficult teens I've worked with over the years are the ones who play the compliance game. They are products of the "discipline" column in table 1. They look nice on the outside, but it masks an interior that is morally weak and two-faced. They've learned how to play the game, but they aren't prepared for life. They may have their parents faked out, because they have been studying them for years and know how to work them; but they are also in danger of lying to themselves. They really aren't prepared to take on life's challenges, though their parents think they are.

Think about it: 80 percent of U.S. high school graduates graduate from the church when they go off to college. That is, eight out of ten kids who were active in their church stop attending church when they hit the university campus.[3]

Why? I think, for one reason, because they can. They are exercising their choice to not go. Eighteen-year-olds revel in their free agent status.

Another reason is that church doesn't seem relevant or cool. When they move to a new city for college, they'd rather spend their time doing something else—like sleeping in. There are lots of parties on Saturday night that make wake-up time on Sunday around noon.

But the main reason, I believe, that first-year college students stop attending church is because they weren't discipled in high school. If a teen has had a mentoring relationship with an adult (whether his parent or someone else), he will be much more likely to be comfortable with adults in the new setting of a different church at college. He will have relational skills and the experience that will lead him to seek out a similar kind of church, even though he may not seek the same kind of discipleship relationship. Once he has tasted of the care, community and growth that occur in real discipleship, he won't go back to church as usual.

Freshmen college students stop attending church because they weren't discipled in high school.

I met a university student who had come to California from the Midwest. He was close to his dad, and a youth ministry volunteer had discipled him in high school. His youth pastor had recommended our church.

"I wanted to come here and check things out. I've heard that your church is like mine back home. You take discipleship and family seriously. I can tell I'll fit right in."

"Do you want to get into our discipleship program?"

"Nah, I'm good. I just want to come here because I can connect with people my age and older, like I did back home."

"Cool." I smiled.

"Yeah, it is."

Eighty-five percent of our kids want a mentor. Seventy percent would like to spend more time with their dad.[4]

As a Gallup research fellow, I have the privilege of working with George Gallup to investigate emerging social issues, particularly those affecting youth and family. Gallup's grasp of the data is commendable. For example:

Surveys clearly show that most Americans place high importance on family and fatherhood. Those among us who have had the blessing of a loving father must reach out to the four in ten children in our society who come home each day from school to fatherless homes. In fact, each of us at this moment might well ask ourselves this question: *Is there a child out there somewhere who deserves the same blessings I received from a father and who needs someone to walk alongside him or her through the travails of youth?* Shouldn't we all be mentors of one kind or another? If we do not reach out to the fatherless children in our nation, we can count on confronting severe societal problems for years to come. More importantly, as people who have experienced the love an earthly father, and the love of God of the universe, can we do less?[5]

"Shouldn't we all be mentors of one kind or another?" It resonates, doesn't it? Why not start at home? Why not start with your child?

DISCONNECTION

Our culture is suffering from a huge disconnect. We are spending significantly less time with friends and neighbors than we used to. It could be that we have shifted time allocated for social encounters to time alone—at the health club, in our home theater or at the bowling alley, or more likely to work more hours to cover the mounting bills.

Parents are not connected with their children. Some kids see their dad only on weekends, though they live in the same house. Adults are disconnected from neighbors and other parents. Teens are not connected with adults in the community. This lack of community has caused teens to feel devalued and forgotten.

"My dad spends more time with his caddy than he does me," complained fifteen year-old Jake, "and I'm on the high school golf team!"

Thirteen-year-old Trish confided, "My mom goes to her health club every day for two hours, but she never has time to take me to the mall, or even for a smoothie. She's just so into herself, and she thinks I'm the one who has the bad it's-all-about-me attitude!"

If a parent is not available, that parent is actually contributing to the emergence of an immoral child.

"My parents are really into the Internet. They both work all day on computers. When they get home, they work some more on computers; then they play on their computers until my bedtime," complained sixteen-year-old Trevor. "About the only time we have to talk is over dinner, but the TV is on, and it's not even a sitcom. I have to talk over Fox News to be heard in my family."

How can children learn from their parents if they aren't available? How can parents mentor kids if they never talk with them? Consider the ramifications of parents' abdicating responsibility for teaching morals to their kids. If a parent is not available or is emotionally tuned out or burned out, that parent is actually contributing to the emergence of an immoral child.

Parents may feed and clothe their child, buy her expensive toys, enroll her in lessons and sports, but if they fail to pass on a sense of right and wrong, they are guilty of moral neglect.

Seizing teachable moments and illustrating with stories, parents can have layers of daily interaction with their children. A generation that genuinely cares for its children would instill morality from the preschool years on and would not back off even during adolescence when they challenge the rules. It may be unpopular to demand certain ethical standards of our kids, but it is necessary.

Sadly, the current generation of parents generally does not seem interested in going to the trouble to have conversations about morals with their children and teens. Some of us have delegated that responsibility to the Sunday school teacher or youth pastor. But we are missing out if we delegate the moral and spiritual development of our children to someone else. We should not "outsource" their moral and spiritual development to another.

Of course it's not easy. Few of us have examples of how to do it. We probably did not see our parents do it. But we do have an example in Jesus. He discipled his followers, some of whom were teenagers and in their early twenties, in the natural course of the day. He didn't have a seminar room with media presentations. He didn't have manuals. He used everyday events to model kingdom principles, and he used common elements to teach spiritual truths. A boy's lunch became an object lesson for faith and recognizing God's ownership of all we have and are. A fruit tree became a "media" presentation of accountability and a reminder that good things come out of a good heart. Even weeds were used to illustrate principles of Christ's kingdom. Jesus told his followers, "Let [the weeds and the wheat] grow together until the harvest. At that time I will tell the harvesters: First collect the weeds and tie them in bundles to be burned; then gather the wheat and bring it into my barn" (Matthew 13:30).

I have weeds in my yard, and I'm trying to think how I can use them to teach moral and spiritual truths! Discipleship in parenting is more a way of thinking, though, than specific steps to follow. It's using the mundane to teach the sublime. It's capturing seemingly meaningless moments and making them opportunities to talk about things that matter.

But we have to be present, and we have to be alert. We can't let days, weeks and months slide by. We have to be intentional and take the initiative. Discipleship doesn't happen by accident. Note Paul's encouragement to his disciples in Thessalonica:

> But we were gentle among you, like a mother caring for her little children. We loved you so much that we were delighted to share with you not only the gospel of God *but our lives as well,* because you had become so dear to us. . . . For you know that we dealt with each of you as a father deals with his own children, encouraging, comforting and urging you to live lives worthy of God, who calls you into his kingdom and glory. (1 Thessalonians 2:7-8, 11-12 NIV)

Discipleship is sharing our lives with our children because they are dear to us. We want them to build their lives around worthy ideals that glorify God.

But sometimes we model the wrong message. Like the time I was trying to teach our daughters to be kind and self-controlled. They were in elementary school and liked to provoke and tease each other. We talked with them about being considerate of each other's feelings and not reacting in anger. "Self-control will keep you out of trouble and from hurting someone's feelings," I said as I sent them to their rooms for a timeout.

A few minutes after their release, our dog, Bingo, made a mess on our new carpet. I freaked out! I grabbed him by the collar and yanked him outside, then grabbed a newspaper, rolled it up and thumped him a few times. He cowered and slithered away with his tail between his legs. I caught my breath and went inside.

"Looks like Daddy needs some self-control," one of the girls said.

THE DEATH OF ALLOWANCES

I've read many of the popular books like *Rich Dad, Poor Dad* and *The*

Millionaire Next Door. I pictured my kids learning how to save, becoming thrifty shoppers, investing prudently and making millions by the time they were thirty, and sharing their wealth with me.

A dad can dream, can't he?

We gave our girls *salaries* instead of allowances because we thought the word *allowance* played into their default setting of entitlement. "Dad, I've kept myself alive for a week; gimme my allowance!" We had a vision of their becoming savvy with money and learning how to live on 80 percent, save 10 percent and give away 10 percent. We even suggested these ratios.

Remember what I said earlier about "model values and teach skills"? Sometimes I really didn't do either of these well. We charged things on credit cards, overextended the budget and had enough in savings for a few meals at Taco Bell.

When Nicole turned sixteen, we went to the bank to open her first checking account. It was a big moment—getting those checks with *her* name on them! When we got home, I presented a quick orientation on how to write checks, how to record them and how to balance the checkbook. She nodded and smiled and waved me off as sixteen-year-olds are adept at doing.

Recently, more than eight years later, I asked Nicole, "Where did I blow it in my modeling or teaching you?" (This is a risky question, not for the faint of heart.)

She thought for a while. "You really didn't teach me how to handle my checking account. I really didn't know how to balance the checkbook, and I didn't learn to budget and I overspent. When I got credit cards in college, it only got worse. I wish you had taught me more."

Looking back, I see that I didn't follow through. Once I got Nicole a checkbook, I thought I was done with this skill. I gave her a tool, but I didn't train her in its use. It's like giving your child a power tool but not showing her how to handle it safely and properly. I think I may have avoided training Nicole more thoroughly regarding finances because at some level I knew I wasn't modeling the best example.

We tend to avoid dealing with the issues in our kids that remind us of our own. And we shouldn't assume that our child understands something just because she says she does—we should test, observe, try again.

My wife and I have learned some lessons about finances in the last few years. And so has Nicole. We're learning to grow together in the area of finances. It's difficult, but in a discipleship-oriented home both parent and child can grow and learn. The emphasis is on the process, not perfection.

Don't be surprised if your child has your hair, your eyes and your foibles.

3

Clarifying Vision

You must have parenting all figured out," said the fortysomething woman at the book table, following my parenting seminar. "I mean you are an author and a family coach, with a graduate degree and all of this experience. Can my kids come live with you?"

I thought of how, on my way out the door to the airport the day before, I had snapped at our teenage daughter for not cleaning up the kitchen. *If she only knew. I don't need one more kid to yell at.*

"I get asked that a lot," I smiled at her, trying to erase the memory of my parental failure, and noticed bags under her eyes. "Depends. How much money would you send with them?"

"All of it! I'm worn out. I'm going to try to apply what you presented today about becoming the relaxed parent—helping my kids do more as I do less. God knows I need to. *The relaxed parent*—it sounds beautiful. You must live in the perfect family."

"No, our home is far from perfect; remember, *I* live there. Our situation is just like yours: messy kids' rooms, makeup and beauty supplies tossed all over the bathroom, towels on the floor, bras hanging from doorknobs, dog messes on the new carpet, bills stacking up, a sink that drains slowly and a toilet that seems to sense when company is in the house. Sound familiar?"

She nodded. "How do you hang in there when you feel like quitting?" She dabbed at a tear forming in her eye.

"I've been there. I've wanted to throw in the towel. I've asked, 'Where does a dad go to resign?' but through it all—through the doctors saying, 'We need to operate on your newborn;' through the panic of losing a three-year-old at Disneyland; through the rough nights of a feverish child, wiping her sweating brow and mopping up the vomit at three a.m. and through those anxious mornings, again at three a.m. wondering *will she make it home safely from the prom?* Through all of those difficulties, I've tried to keep my perspective. In spite of the emotions and the temptation to freak out, I struggle to keep the end in mind. To focus on the vision I have for my children. Sometimes I actually can."

"How do you do that?"

"I try to remember a story I read years ago by Gordon MacDonald in his book *The Effective Father,*" I confided. I gave her my best recollection of the following quote:

Among the legends is the tale of a medieval sidewalk superintendent who asked three stonemasons on a construction project what they were doing. The first replied, "Why, I'm laying bricks." The second one replied, "I'm building a wall." But the third laborer demonstrated his vision and genuine esteem for his work. When the superintendent asked, "What are you building?" he buoyantly exclaimed, "I am raising a great cathedral, which will have giant spires pointing to the heavens. To the glory of God!" . . .

Pose that same question to any two fathers concerning their role in the family, and you are liable to get the same kind of contrast. The first may say, "I am supporting my family." But the second may see things differently and say, "I am *raising* children to the glory of God." The former looks at his job as *putting bread on the table*. But the latter see things in God's perspective: he is *participating in the shaping of lives.*[1]

Vision is seeing life from God's point of view. It will give you perseverance when you need it. Vision gives you perspective. It will help you spend your time and energy on the right things.

Vision is seeing life from God's point of view.

WHAT DO YOU SEE?

Are you a successful parent? How will you know if you are?

Parenting is controversial and complex. Experts don't agree on theories or practice. You can pick up one book at the bookstore and it will advocate permissiveness. The book next to it promotes tight control. What's a parent to do?

A 2005 nationwide survey of parents conducted by the Barna Group offers some surprising insights into what parents in our society want to see in their children. In effect, the findings reveal parents' vision for their children. By far the top-rated outcome at 39 percent was getting a good education. Helping the child to feel loved was the second most frequently mentioned outcome at 24 percent, and 22 percent prioritized enabling their child to have a meaningful relationship with Jesus Christ. A little lower on the list was "helping my child feel happy" at 10 percent. But what caught my eye was way down the list at 4 percent: "helping them establish appropriate moral values."[2]

Only 4 percent of the parents surveyed thought it was important to help their kids develop moral values. More than twice as many parents were more concerned with making their kids *happy* than with seeing their kids be moral.

In case you are wondering, the sample was 1,004 adults, and over a third described themselves as "born again Christians." So it's obvious that most Christian parents are not sure how to raise their kids in a way that is distinctive from families that don't claim any faith. Most of us are suffering from blurry vision. Perhaps we're too busy or we don't have role models that work for us with this generation. It could be that we are majoring on the minors. We are putting too much emphasis on things that in the long haul won't matter.

If we are seeking to disciple our children, the goal isn't their happiness but helping them prepare for life and make wise choices. One of the crucial goals parents often forget is imparting a vision to their child—helping her discover her purpose and see herself as a significant member of a larger community, contributing to a greater cause.

Sadly, according to the Barna study, parents have blurry vision. Most parents are chasing after the wrong goal. They reason, *I need to work long hours to provide enrichment for my kids.* Is it any wonder that most parents don't feel successful at home? It's easier to work long hours at the office than come home and deal with the uncertainties of intimate relationships. Sociologist Arlie Hochschild of the University of California at Berkeley notes:

> Despite its aggravations, many people like being at work. They feel rewarded on the job. Their friends are there; so are their social lives, their support systems. At work, people feel more appreciated and competent. The result is that families get short-changed. Growing numbers of women feel torn, guilty and stressed by their long hours at work, but they're ambivalent about cutting back on those hours.[3]

Many parents are climbing the ladder of success and dragging their kids behind them, only to discover that the ladder is leaning against the wrong building. The ladder is leaning against the fun house from a traveling carnival. Tomorrow the structure will be gone! Happiness for our children is too elusive a goal.

Education, love and happiness for our kids are noble goals, but they shouldn't consume 90 percent of our time, energy and emotion. I see the shock in parents' faces when I say, "If your kid gets C's and a few D's and is honest, kind and works hard, he'll be fine."

> *Don't stress. Pray. The same Holy Spirit that is in you is in your children.*

Heresy! I can tell that's what they're thinking.

I want my daughters to be educated. I want them to feel loved. And I want them to be happy. But there is something more important.

I want them to know and love God.

Okay, so that *is* a big one, actually the most important one. If a child receives Christ, he becomes a new creation in Christ, old things pass away and all things become new (2 Corinthians 5:17). Our children need to become more like Christ. We see immature foibles in them that we'd like to extinguish. If we rely on only our own efforts, it can be very difficult; but with God's help, working from the inside out, it's possible.

I like to tell Christian parents, "Don't stress. Pray. The same Holy Spirit that is in you is in them. Pray that he'll do his work."

This book is about cooperating with God to develop qualities and life skills in the lives of our children. It starts with their knowing and loving God.

Researcher George Barna wrestles with an alarming problem: "For years we have reported research findings showing that born again adults think and behave very much like everyone else. It often seems that their faith makes very little difference in their life. This new study helps explain why that is: believers do not train their children to think or act any differently."[4] Before we can pass along vision to our children, we must have one for ourselves as parents.

Many of us view ourselves as being successful, but I would submit that we are successful at the wrong things! No wonder many of us are frustrated parents. Instead of painting a facade on the front of our home, we'd be better off spending our time and energy strengthening the foundation. It's no good to have a home with curb appeal but a crumbling foundation.

The foundation for vision is who we are in Christ. When our daughters were little, Suzanne and I sat down and wrote our aims for parenting. I call it "the Target, or what we want our children to be like at eighteen years old."

We prayed about these qualities and life skills and committed them to writing. They have guided us in our parenting. In the fog and fatigue, they gave clarity and renewal. When we came to that inevitable fork in the road—"deal with it or let it go?"—we simply had to pull out the Target and see what the long-term aim was. This doesn't mean we were perfect or followed the Target every time, but it does mean we weren't meandering all over the course slicing or hooking with every drive or putt.

THE TARGET

What We Want Our Children to Be Like at Eighteen Years Old

Spiritual   To have a growing and vibrant faith in Christ

	To be able to explain and defend their faith
	To be in community with other believers the same age
Social	To be able to make wise decisions about friends and activities
	To be able to relate to a wide variety of people in diverse situations
Physical	To be in good health and maintain habits of an active lifestyle
	To preserve their virginity until they are married
	To live a substance-abuse-free lifestyle
Emotional	To feel capable, confident of self and of God-given abilities
	To draw boundaries (not be taken advantage of by others—personal courage)
Mental	To be prepared for opportunities encountered in the future
	To be lifelong learners and perform up to their potential academically
	To think critically and biblically with a Christian worldview
Character	To be honest, just, dependable, forgiving, compassionate and generous
Life Skills	To develop skills in finances, vocational planning, ministry involvement, cooking, cleaning, car maintenance and personal organization, etc.

(See appendix two for a more extensive Target.)

Keeping your Target handy will help you evaluate what to do when you encounter inevitable parenting challenges. For instance, when we moved to Thousand Oaks from Orange County, we chose to buy a house in a neighborhood where our girls could walk to school. We wanted them to have the exercise and the experience with neighborhood friends, and we didn't want to have to drive them! We chose a school where they would develop friends of diverse ethnic backgrounds. Over the years, both developed long-lasting relationships with friends of racial and national diversity. To help model compassion and service, our family vacation at spring break often would be in Mexico for a week, building homes and leading Bible clubs for children.

Each element of the Target becomes a measurable goal. They can be used for self-assessment: *Are we on target? Have we done anything recently to develop compassion? At what age should we teach them how to cook?*

See how it goes? The Target can become a customized checklist for parenting. Of course, make sure it does not become a cumbersome, legalistic burden; use it simply as a diagnostic tool to see if you are on course, a sort of GPS—Good Parenting Sense.

Creating a Target helps establish in your mind a preferred picture of what you'd like your child to become. It is your *vision* of what kind of person you want your daughter or son to mature to become. Your children are more likely to become persons of vision if they have grown up in a home that believes in and reinforces vision.

DEVELOPING A VISION FOR YOUR CHILD

Have you discussed with your spouse the qualities and skills you would like your children to have when they reach eighteen? Have you talked with God about your plans and desires for your children? Have you evaluated your practices and plans in light of biblical principles? Are you modeling the values you want your child to emulate?

Parents demonstrate faith in God when they are willing to submit their highest hopes for their children to him. Obeying God in the unseen areas means allowing him to have influence over your dreams—both for yourself and for your children.

"Now faith is being sure of what we hope for and certain of what we do not see" (Hebrews 11:1 NIV). You have the opportunity to build your family's faith on a foundation of prayer. Prayer helps us imagine our children's future with confidence because we know that they won't walk alone—God will be with them.

Faith cannot be manipulated or manufactured. It is a response from within us, orchestrated by God. It is his supernatural work within us that generates our ability to trust him with our lives and our children's lives.

> *Parents demonstrate faith in God when they submit their highest hopes for their children to him.*

Record in writing your hopes for your children. Pray about them daily. Ask God to help you remember your vision for your children and to have his creativity and consistency to help your children progress toward the Target.

Godly, healthy and balanced children don't happen by accident, as Tim Kimmel reminds us: "It takes a lot more than good intentions to leave a legacy of love. The best intentions have a tough time competing with the relentless pressures of culture. We have to be focused and strategic. Good intentions that aren't followed by specific actions are just empty words."[5] Raising kids with vision demands that we have a clear picture of what we want them to become. It means defining the Target specifically, objectively and reasonably. When we define what we are aiming for, we are more likely to hit it.

If we can picture the bull's-eye, we are more likely to hit it.

Further, if we can't agree on what we are trying to accomplish as parents, our parenting is destined to fail. But when we define the aim in advance, it helps reduce conflict between us, because we agree on what we are aiming at. It also reduces anxiety because it has reduced confusion. By having an objective for our parenting with specific qualities and skills in mind, we alleviate a lot of our parental fear. We can relax in the reality that we are gradually progressing toward the Target.

> *If we can't agree on what we are trying to accomplish as parents, we are destined to fail.*

ARROWS UNLEASHED

We've been talking about developing a Target for your kids. No, I didn't say, "Use your kids as a target!"—although you've probably felt like that on numerous days! To develop kids with vision, we need to be parents with vision. What is your vision for your kids? How will you know if you achieve it?

The psalmist compares children to arrows:

Sons are a heritage from the LORD,
　children a reward from him.
Like arrows in the hands of a warrior
　are sons born in one's youth.
Blessed is the man
　whose quiver is full of them. (Psalm 127:3-5 NIV)

Note that children aren't a curse—they are a *reward*. They are seen as assets that help us in battle. (In these days of PC—politically correct—behavior, military metaphors are not considered "appropriate," especially within a discussion of family issues. But I think that the biblical wisdom literature has it right. These texts have stood the test of time. I doubt that contemporary PC slogans will still be quoted three thousand years from now!)

If children are like arrows, they need to be aimed in the right direction—toward the Target. Our continent feels the impact of children who have not been pointed toward the targets of personal responsibility and compassion. There are children who shoot and kill other children. They are arrows without direction. An unaimed arrow is a dangerous thing. A child without direction is just as dangerous.

As I see it, there are two kinds of directional problems with our arrow children: those who haven't been aimed and those who haven't been released. Our role as parent-archers is to aim our children toward the bull's-eye of righteousness and wisdom, create tension by pulling back on the string, then release. A failure to release will have the same result as not aiming: we will miss the target.

Know your target.

Aim.

Pull back—create tension.

Release. *Let go.*

What if my kids make foolish choices?

Let go.

What if they don't go the distance?

Let go.

What happens if a gust blows them off course?

Let go.

What if my aim is off?

Let go.

The point of Christian parenting isn't keeping the arrows in the quiver; it's using them, which means releasing them. Yes, there are hundreds of things that could go wrong (and you have stressed about most of them). But you have to let go. You can't run alongside the arrow, trying to maintain contact and redirect it with a quick touch or by blowing on it. For an arrow to fly, you have to release it.

DEVELOPING YOUR CHILD'S VISION

Point your kids in the right direction—
   when they're old they won't be lost. (Proverbs 22:6 *The Message*)

An expert archer will pull an arrow from his quiver and stare down the shaft, noticing the texture and unique properties of the wood's natural grain. He will then rest the arrow on the bow, making adjustments for the wind and the distance and location of the target. He will position each arrow differently, depending on the variations. One arrow might be slightly tilted up; another might be pointed slightly down. If the wind is blowing from the north, the archer may compensate by positioning the arrow on the rest with a slight pitch. He will aim his arrow toward the bull's-eye. A skilled archer studies the variations among arrows, notices the wind and makes adjustments for each so that he can hit the bull's-eye.

A skilled parent does the same thing.

The right direction or "the way he should go" (Proverbs 22:6 NIV) doesn't mean a prescribed path, as in "my way or the highway." It isn't a formula that, if followed, will produce the perfect kid. Many parents focus on their shooting technique, believing they must be consistent and follow "the right way" to be successful. They are concentrating on pulling back the bowstring, but they have forgotten to sight-in their target. Parents who always try to parent "the right way" may be very frustrated when a child veers off course. In this situation the parent archers have not considered the natural bent of the arrow or the winds of the environment (culture). They have focused only on the bow—not the arrow, nor the target.

The bull's eye is who we envision our child to become.

Consider using your target to develop vision for and within your child. Use it to impart a preferred future to your child. It is one of the visionary tools you can use with your family, along with your top values and a family mission statement.

Our family mission statement, for instance, is "The Smiths exist to love each other and advance God's timeless principles and his kingdom on earth." Based on this, we can say that one of our family's core values is to love each other unconditionally. Another one is that we will be active with our faith and willing to take risks. A third might be that we base our family practice, rules and priorities on God's timeless principles revealed in Scripture. Our ultimate goal as a family is to advance God's kingdom (not be comfortable, or accumulate wealth, or become famous). Check out appendix one for tips on developing *your* family mission statement.

As we look to our children's future, we should focus on the things that we can influence and hold loosely those we can't. We can't plan (nor should we) their specific career or decide whom they marry or even if they marry. We can't plan for them to live near us or for them to attend church. But we can model what's important to us and train them in the skills that they will need.

What's important to you? What would your children say is important to you? It doesn't take long to get to the practical realities of life. If you have never stated your values clearly, your children may assume that to you the most important things are to be comfortable, accumulate wealth, have nice kids and have a good reputation. These aren't bad things. They just don't excite vision in the hearts and minds of our kids.

Our kids are desperate for vision. They are craving purpose. Millennials, as postmoderns, yearn to be part of a grand story. Their hearts long to be characters in a story that matters—one with a creative design, passionate characters and a noble mission. Tragedies, materialism and the hectic pace of our culture diminish the craving, but it isn't destroyed. *The longing for transcendence* is a passion to be something larger than myself and out of the ordinary.

A child with vision doesn't get trapped in the mundane. There is something he is shooting for. He has ideals and goals that inspire him. With an internal sense of purpose and a clear vision of what he wants to become, he is motivated to pursue his aims.

Vision breeds motivation. Kids' key motivations can be summed up as *AIM*.

- *Adventure.* Extreme sports, music videos, hedonism and the beer-commercial mentality express kids' longing for excitement. However, unhealthy expressions should not lead us to discount this valid need.

- *Intimacy.* With over 50 percent of Millennials growing up as children of divorce,[6] they have a huge need to know the inmost character and essence of a person and to be known by another. They are crying out to be included. They don't want to be left out.

- *Meaning.* Our kids are looking for clarity and significance. Growing up in a relativistic, naturalistic culture has left them longing for purpose and an understanding of where they came from and why they are here.

Our kids want to be part of an adventure—a movement or a cause. They want to pursue ideas that are grand and beyond themselves, like racial equality, peace, a clean environment and no war. They see themselves contributing to a world of new hope and sense of purpose.

A family that pursues adventure might take a trip to another country or across town to experience a different culture. They might sign up to serve in a homeless shelter or to help at a crisis pregnancy center. A family that is adventurous takes measured risks, knowing that doing so will enhance the growth of parents and children.

Our children are eager for intimacy. They want to be part of a caring community. They want to know and be known. Families that understand the value of intimacy model committed relationships within the family and with friends. They make time to be with each other. The parents model intimacy by belonging to small groups and maintaining long-term friendships. One of the best resources we can pass along to our kids is the ability to keep and grow friendships through the good times and the bad.

Our children are desperate for meaning. They want to know why they are here, who they are and what they can contribute. A family with a sense of meaning is working to establish a family mission statement. They are operating from a core of shared values, and they have open discussions on how they can make their behavior match their values. A family with meaning challenges the nihilism and hopelessness that are common in our culture. They know that a clear vision gives purpose and direction to life.

ADJUSTING YOUR VISION

I wear contacts. Without them I can't see beyond a foot away. My world is very blurry without visual correction. I can't think straight without my contacts or glasses; I get anxious and feel helpless.

Our kids are the same way, regardless of how good their physical eyesight is. They feel nervous and vulnerable, without clear vision.

They can't see far into the future. It's blurry. It's unknown. They've never been there.

That's where we come in as parents. It is our job to help them see beyond what they can currently see. We are like contacts that help our children correct their vision and see further than what they would naturally see. It is our job to clarify our children's vision.

Have you helped your child develop her vision? Have you worked on her AIM? What plans do you have to fulfill her quest for *adventure*? How can you help her discover healthy, intentional *intimacy*? And what might you do to enhance her sense of *meaning*?

With a clear vision of who they are in Christ, your children can handle a variety of temptations, assaults and detours. They won't be focused on *what* is around them but on *who* is inside them. The most important thought a Christian can entertain is *Who am I in Christ?*

Consider using the following biblical concepts to help your children develop vision for their life. Pray about them. Discuss them with your children. Memorize them together. Post them on your fridge.

Design

- God created us according to his master plan:

You made all the delicate, inner parts of my body
     and knit me together in my mother's womb.
Thank you for making me so wonderfully complex!
     Your workmanship is marvelous—and how well I know it.
(Psalm 139:13-14 NLT)

- We were created by intelligent design rather than by evolution through natural selection. We aren't mistakes; we are masterpieces. We are creations of worth.

Destiny

- We discover our purpose and future in relationship with God: "'For I know the plans I have for you,' says the LORD. 'They are plans for good and not for disaster, to give you a future and a hope'" (Jeremiah 29:11 NLT).
- Each of us has a soul with a unique shape that fits God. Each of us has a unique, creative contribution to make. We are God's people.

Duty

- We can offer service to God and others.
- God has created us with skills and talents that will benefit others: "God has given gifts to each of you from his great variety of spiritual gifts. Manage them well so that God's generosity can flow through you" (1 Peter 4:10 NLT).
- We are valuable to the mission and purpose God has planned. Our service has eternal consequences.

When your thirteen-year-old is stressed about zits, body hair and the size of his feet, help him understand that he is *fearfully and wonderfully made.* He's just in process.

When your nine-year-old doesn't make the cut for the dance production, help her to understand that even though it's disappointing and sad, it isn't a disaster. God has plans for us, even when we face difficulties and disappointments.

And when your seven-year-old feels left out because he's the youngest, help him to see that everyone has something to contribute. Help him to discover the unique competency that he can contribute to the family. He might be "the best dog washer in the family," or perhaps he makes "the tastiest microwave macaroni and cheese."

Give your child a sense of purpose with a clear vision.

4

Embracing Authenticity

There are times as a dad that I have to rely on my acting skills, as pathetic as they are. There are times when I really don't know what to do or what to say as a "father figure."

So I fake it. Sometimes I pull it off. But not all the time.

When Brooke was about seven years old, I was disciplining her for some misbehavior I don't even remember now. (We parents tend to block these things out. It's probably a good thing.)

Anyway, I'm trying to be like a TV dad and not lose my cool, but my voice is cracking, my blood pressure is peaking and the little vein on the side of my forehead is popping out. I'm trying to be chill, but I'm turning pink.

After a few minutes of my serious and hopefully life-changing lecture, Brooke starts to laugh.

I'm furious. I'm trying to be Superdad and she's smacking Kryptonite in my face. "What's so funny?" I yell.

"Your face is funny, Daddy. The thing on your head is popping out and you sound funny, and you're as pink as my Puffalump."

I wanted to lash out, but somehow I was able to temporarily get into her second-grade world and see what I looked like from her perspective. *It was funny!* This grown man, six feet and two hundred pounds of volcanic activity—that *she* had caused—was turning various shades of red and purple and sounding like a pubescent thirteen-year-old.

Once I got a glimpse of what I looked like to her, it made me laugh. It really was funny and it was temporary. Somehow I was able to see that this was simply a season—an episode in a much larger story. I was trying to make it *the* story, but it wasn't. It was only a small episode.

Don't take yourself too seriously as a parent.

Brooke helped me see this. We laughed, talked about the issue, instituted some consequence and went on with life.

There's a huge lesson here: Don't take yourself too seriously as a parent. Your kids may be laughing at you; try laughing with them sometimes. Another lesson I began learning at that point: Don't ruin your relationship over an issue of discipline. You can influence your child if you have a relationship with her, but you can't if you are alienated from her. Don't sacrifice the relationship over one area of misbehavior. Kids will act up. They will make mistakes. They will disappoint us. They will act immature, impulsive and irrational. They'll act like children.

In the midst of our child's misbehavior, we want to communicate, *You are important to me, and I will always love you. We'll get through this together.*

I'm not saying be permissive and ignore the misbehavior. I am saying the child is more than just her behavior—good or bad.

Give up on the notion of raising the perfect child. Give up on the notion of trying to be the perfect parent, and settle for being an authentic one.

MIDWESTERN NICE

Last winter I was asked to present a parenting seminar in Minnesota. I don't know what it is, but every winter I'm asked to go to Minnesota, Wisconsin or Michigan. I guess ice fishing isn't enough and people need something else to do at night. If you are from snow country I'm sure it's not a big deal to you, but I'm from sunny Southern California and I'm not used to anything below fifty degrees.

I like the folks in the Midwest. They are so polite and hospitable. I mentioned this at dinner and my hostess said, "Ah, that's Minnesota Nice, don't ya know?"

"What's that?" I asked.

"It's an unwritten rule that you have to be friendly up front. Take time to smile, greet folks, chat a little, then go about your work, ya know."

"No wonder. That explains why everyone is friendly. I didn't think the snow cheered up everyone."

"But it's only at a superficial level," she explained. "It's not always sincere, and it doesn't mean you want the conversation to go further. It's just settin' a friendly mood."

"*Minnesota Nice.* It seems like that style prevails in Wisconsin and Michigan too."

"Ya, shoor," she nodded her blonde head, "but we Minnysotens pride ourselves on our niceness. It's our state motto, 'Everybody be nice.'"

I think she was kidding, but I'm not sure. "How will I know when I see it?"

"When someone says 'interesting' to you, they really don't mean it. What they mean is *That's the biggest crock I've heard all winter,* but they don't say it, don't ya know, because that wouldn't be nice."

"Lots of parents said that to me after the seminar." I was rattled.

She just nodded and chewed her roast beef.

I was intrigued. "What else?"

She sipped her water, then said, "When they end a sentence with 'alrighty then,' it means 'That's it, I'm done with you, let's get along to our work or something else.'"

"I thought it was a cheery, bouncy saying—something Santa's happy elves say as they work at the North Pole: *alrighty then*. It's not, though?"

She shook her head.

"I heard a lot of that too. I thought they were simply being polite, and at one level they were, but at another they were saying *Enough*, right?"

> *Give up on the notion of trying to be the perfect parent, and settle for being an authentic one.*

"You betcha . . . Want seconds?" She handed me the roast beef and mashed potatoes. "Your presentation was *interesting*," she cracked with a droll smirk.

Our kids don't need us to be cheerfully superficial. They don't need cheerleaders; they need parents. We don't have to be Super Parents or always be serious. We can laugh, have fun and most of all, be real with our kids. We are what our children need—the real us, not some polished, polite, *nice* parent.

LAURA'S LEGACY

Laura was a single mom with a seventeen-year-old son. For his eighteenth birthday she wanted to pass on wisdom from a male perspective. She contacted family members, coaches and male friends and asked them to write about an experience in which they learned about life. It might be a failure, a success or simply an insight. She compiled these in a notebook and added her own introduction. She wrote that as Jason's mom she couldn't teach him all he needed to know about being a man.

Since his father had left many years prior, Jason had had no regular male role model in his life. Laura didn't try to be a father to him. She acknowledged her inability to do so, but with the wisdom journal she provided a set of strong masculine voices to her son at a time that he needed them. When his eighteenth birthday came, she cooked his favorite meal and presented the legacy notebook.

Jason reads and rereads the notes from his mentors. They have become a treasure to him.

It all started with Laura's being authentic. She didn't try to be something she wasn't. She was herself and modeled authenticity, leading to a significant, positive impact on her son.

STATUS QUO = THE MESS WE'Z IN

Sometimes it's difficult to be authentic. It's challenging to provide a positive example for our kids. A lot of parents I talk to sense pressure. They feel that they are under the critical gaze of others. They are afraid to be real.

Something is wrong. It used to be that we had backup. If the kid acted up in the grocery store, the other shoppers would support your discipline or threat of it. Now, if you try to stop the misbehavior in public, you have squinty-eyed judges with their finger on their cell phones, ready to speed-dial Children's Protective Services. I'm not saying to ignore obvious cases of abuse, but I am saying that most parents are afraid to discipline their children in public.

Something is broken. We can no longer rely on the traditional support systems—extended families, neighbors, the church, community programs and schools—that at one time reinforced our attempts to nurture and train our kids. Our society isn't providing what our kids need to flourish.

So it comes down to us—the parents. We have to pick up the ball and run with it. We have to create new support systems. We have to have a plan and stick with it and not give in to the distractions and the temptation to be a wimpy parent.

Our society isn't providing what our kids need to flourish.

It begins with us. Will your child become a civil, sociable, God-fearing member of the community, or will he turn out to be rude, self-involved, emotionally weak hedonist? The values you model in your daily dealings with your child will determine the result. Your authenticity will help pass along your values to your child.

Our example is critical. *Everything* we do teaches our kids something about life and becoming a mature individual.

Strong parents produce strong kids. Weak parents produce weak kids. Kids pick up what they grow up with. A child who manipulates her parents by whining, throwing fits and sulking won't develop the emotional strength to deal with disappointment, waiting, frustration and boredom and will become more lethal in her teens. How will she have the inner strength and self-control to resist cheating, sex and substance abuse?

It seems to me that that we have shifted to an extreme in our culture. We are held hostage by a cultural climate suggesting that moral training of our kids is inappropriate. Take a look around. Most kids today don't have a clear, internalized sense of right and wrong. They don't respect rules. They don't respect authority. And they don't per-

ceive the consequences of their unethical behavior. They may have
refined their manipulative techniques and know how to put the right
"spin" on things, but their duplicity
doesn't produce integrity. Integrity is essential because it has a "what-you-see-is-
what-you-get" quality to it.

Our culture is starving for genuine
community. Where there is no pretense.
Where we can get below the veneer. A
person is the same on the *inside* as she is
on the *outside*. Without authenticity we
don't have integrity. Without integrity, we
can't have genuine community, because

Strong parents produce strong kids. Weak parents produce weak kids.

everyone is posing. Authentic community is described in Paul's
words to the Colossians:

> Don't lie to one another. You're done with that old life. It's like
> a filthy set of ill-fitting clothes you've stripped off and put in the
> fire. Now you're dressed in a new wardrobe. Every item of your
> new way of life is custom-made by the Creator, with his label
> on it. All the old fashions are now obsolete. Words like Jewish
> and non-Jewish, religious and irreligious, insider and outsider,
> uncivilized and uncouth, slave and free, mean nothing. From
> now on *everyone is defined by Christ, everyone is included in
> Christ*. (Colossians 3:9-11 *The Message*, emphasis added)

In the first century, for Paul to say that labels like *Jew* and *insider*
meant *nothing* was revolutionary. He lived in a very class-oriented society. One's class and position were very important. As postmodern
Americans living with two hundred years of democracy under our
leather liberty belt, with an eagle on the buckle, it's difficult for us to

understand. We've heard "all men are created equal" hundreds of times.

Authenticity is possible when we have Christ in common. "Everyone is included by Christ." The ground is level at the foot of the cross. Nobody gets to brag that they are in the club because of connections, wealth or the charity work they've done. We get into the "club" by admitting that we are sinners, that we have failed morally.

POSER PARENTS

Some parents are breathlessly sprinting on a treadmill, trying to be the perfect parents. Their obsession is to project a flawless life. This is an enemy to authenticity. It is toxic to our kids. Tim Kimmel calls it "image-control parenting":

> This is a checklist method of parenting that is part of the seduction of legalism. My parents employed this kind of parenting model in the early years of raising their kids. Image-control parenting assumes that people will know you are a good Christian parent raising nice Christian offspring by your church attendance, the way you dress (or don't dress), the way you cut your hair (or don't), the words and expressions you use (or don't use), the schools you attend (or don't attend), the movies you see (or don't see), the amount of Scripture you can quote, the version of the Bible you read, and the kinds of treats you give out for Halloween (if you participate at all). The problem with this form of parenting is not in the things these parents either do or don't do. For the most part, these are well-meaning people trying to make good choices, but they make them for the *wrong reasons!* Doing good things for wrong reasons consistently brings unfavorable results. Unfortunately, kids can tell

when we are living by a checklist rather than trusting God to lead us.[1]

Trying to maintain an image as a parent is impossible, and it's not healthy either. Just when we are looking good and have it all figured out, the little terrorists come along and blow things up! Kids have a way of revealing false pretenses—especially in their parents.

> *Trying to maintain an image as a parent is impossible, and it's not healthy either.*

Trying to maintain an image is exhausting. It requires lots of emotional and physical energy to maintain the façade. Some of the most fatigued parents I know are the ones who subscribe to image-control parenting. Acting takes a lot of adrenaline and concentration. These parents are acting their way through the day—acting like the perfect mom or the perfect dad.

The pursuit of the perfect image is insidious; it is also toxic. It is toxic because it establishes deception as one of the operational values of the home:

- "In all cases, look good."
- "No matter what, don't shame our family name."
- "We are a Christian family and want to be a good witness to others. We must live *above reproach*."

Now, I admit, that last admonition doesn't sound so noxious; but what some parents mean by "good witness" is "we let lost people see us, but we really don't have friendships with them because it might rub off on us"—their badness, that is.

And what they mean by "living above reproach" is to live perfect, untainted lives that follow the humanly generated rules for holiness and also make others look like corrupt scoundrels.

Looking good on the outside and not having it together on the inside leads to deception as the standard operating procedure in the home. It becomes an unspoken but practiced value.

I've had parents complain to me that their kids lie to them, only to later find out from the kids that the parents lie at the movie box office to get the under-twelve children's price. And that their parents are concerned about their behavior not for the sake of the child but for how their behavior reflected on the parent. Image-control parenting is a breeding ground for hypocrisy.

BEING REAL IN A FAKE WORLD

Our kids, the Millennials, are desperate for authentic relationships. They're familiar with all the hype, the slick marketing and the promises. They are looking for someone to underpromise and overdeliver. That person should be you, their parent.

They know you aren't perfect. I can prove it.

Do they know your hot buttons? Do they know how to work you? Can they get you to react?

I thought so; my kids do too.

So give up the notion of the perfect act, and settle for being authentic. When you are authentic, you create an atmosphere of truth and grace. Within that environment your child will grow to become authentic as well.

This is what Paul had in mind when he continued in his letter to the Colossians:

So, chosen by God for this new life of love, dress in the wardrobe God picked out for you: compassion, kindness, humility, quiet strength, discipline. Be even-tempered, content with second place, quick to forgive an offense. Forgive as quickly and completely as the Master forgave you. And regardless of what else you put on, wear love. It's your basic, all-purpose garment. Never be without it. (Colossians 3:12-14 *The Message*)

These are qualities of authentic relationships. Note that they aren't a checklist of culturally approved behaviors or standards of the Perfect Parent Club. They are assets for effective relationships as well as Christlike character qualities.

We can be authentic if we are humble. We can be authentic when we have quiet strength. We don't have to call attention to ourselves. We don't have to look marvelous. Authenticity helps us not react. We aren't trying to hide something, so if a challenge comes along, we don't have to react. Instead, we are even-tempered and self-controlled.

Authentic people don't have to win. Not everything is a competition to them. They are quick to forgive—remembering God's grace and forgiveness for them.

Authentic people can love others because they have learned to love themselves. They have learned to accept themselves, their strengths and their weaknesses. They have an accurate assessment of themselves.

THE TREE HOUSE

Several years ago at Mount Hermon Conference Center, I heard Chuck Swindoll speak on authenticity. He told the story of three kids who made a tree house out of scrap lumber. When they finished, they stood back and admired their work.

"We need to have some rules," said eight-year-old Tommy.

"Why do we need rules?" asked seven-year-old Latisha.

"'Cuz it's our tree house and I don't want nobody in it but us," he explained.

"What kind of rules, Tommy?" asked six-year-old Pablo.

"I dunno. I just don't want somebody bossin' me around in our tree house. But I don't want as many rules as my mom has for me." Tommy scratched his head.

"And I don't want people thinking I'm nothin' 'cuz I'm little," Pablo specified.

"I got an idea! Wait here, I'll be right back," called out Latisha. She ran to her house.

About five minutes later she returned with a sign made from the side of a cardboard box. On the brown corrugated paper, in black marker she had written:

Nobody act big.
Nobody act little.
Everybody act medium.

I think Latisha understands authenticity. When we "act big"—like we are better than others—authenticity is impossible; others are put off by us, and they don't want anything to do with us.

When we "act little," we communicate that we aren't worth knowing. We falsely believe that others wouldn't like to get to know us. We falsely believe that others are more together than we are.

But when we "act medium"—not too big or too little—we are ushering in the possibility of authenticity.

We want to be authentic, and we want our kids to be so as well, because authenticity leads to closeness. We want to be close to our sons and daughters. Healthy parents replace physical closeness with emotional closeness as their child matures. When your child is an infant, you are always holding her, touching her and being with her. But as she grows older and prepares to attend two hours of preschool, you replace some of the physical closeness with emotional closeness. "Mommy will be with you all day. Right here." And you point to her heart.

Authenticity allows for closeness with our children even through the teen years and into the college years. There's something about authentic people that attracts us to them. I don't fully understand this, but I do understand the principle in reverse. If I encounter an engaging person who I sense is fake, I avoid him at all costs. You know what I'm talking about.

JAMIE'S WORLD

"If people only knew what he was really like," fifteen-year-old Jamie fumed. "He's such a poser. He's a goody-goody at church, but at home he's mean, selfish, impatient and angry."

I couldn't believe my ears. The Jim I knew was outgoing, on the church board and a talented public speaker. "There's always two sides to the story, isn't there?"

"Well, no one has ever heard my side, until now. Thanks for listening."

"Sure. I'm learning to not judge the book by the cover or the person by their church-lady or church-man persona."

"It's fake. He's a hypocrite! Why should I have to obey him? I don't respect him. He tells me to follow all his freakin' rules and he's out there breaking all of the commandments!"

I filed away the "all of the commandments" comment for later. "What bugs you the most about him?"

"He lies. He uses all of this sweet, syrupy spiritual talk around church but swears and yells at us at home. He's fakin' people out, and I can't stand him."

It turns out Jamie was right. Sometimes kids rebel against a parent because they sense that something is not true. It's actually healthy when they do. It keeps them from becoming part of the toxic system.

Within months, everyone in town discovered that Jim was indeed a poser. His public faith did not match his home and business life. He was having an affair, and his greed had led to a lack of ethics and breaking the law. It landed him in jail. He lost his business, his reputation and his family.

Hypocrisy destroys a family.

Authenticity strengthens a family.

IN PRAISE OF MEDIOCRITY

I am very familiar with the kind of parents who buy parenting books and go to seminars. They are generally good parents trying to become *great* parents. This is frustrating, because the parents who need help the most often don't seek any kind of input or help.

But I know that a lot of you, dear parents reading this book, are recovering perfectionists. It's okay, you can admit it. We are talking about authenticity in this chapter, so let's get real.

At my seminars I like to ask the parents to complete this sentence: "If it's worth doing, it is . . ."

> *Affirm progress and don't expect perfection.*

And they always get it! They chime in together: "Worth doing well, or not at all."

Then I ask, "Where did you learn this?"

They all say, "From my parents."

With diplomacy and sensitivity, I respond, "Your parents were wrong!"

Think about it. If something is worth doing—if its doing has inherent worth—it is worth doing even *poorly*.

Any attempt is noble as long as it's going in the right direction. It doesn't have to be perfect to have value.

Sometimes we can't learn to do something well unless we try. We learn from trial and error. If it's worth doing, it's worth doing poorly! Three cheers for mediocrity!

I know this is extremely annoying to you perfectionists. But if we are going to teach our kids values, we need to give them some training wheels. We need to let them have a few crashes and a few bandaged knees. It is better for them to learn while they are under our protection and watchful eye than to have to learn in the big, bad world when they are on their own. The home is the place where they can learn without the full impact of negative consequences. They can learn through trial and error without being devastated. Try to affirm progress and don't expect perfection.

What your kids need is you.

Your kids are eager for a relationship with you. Psychology, accomplishments, materialism and the best enrichment opportunities aren't what they need. What your kids need is *you*.

SEVEN TIPS FOR DEVELOPING AUTHENTICITY IN YOUR CHILD

1. Give up the notion of and the attempts at being the perfect parent.

2. Tell your child an age-appropriate story from your childhood or teen years, when you learned an important lesson from failure.

3. Share with your child biographies of influential people and role models who failed many times before they had success. (Examples include Abraham Lincoln, Albert Einstein, Marie Curie and many well-known missionaries.)

4. Avoid labeling people based on externals like race, looks, nationality, disabilities, religion or political party. Instead, remind yourself and your child that God looks at the heart (1 Samuel 16:7). A person's heart is what matters, not their "shell."

5. When your children misbehave, temper the discipline if they are truthful. Say, "If you are honest about your misbehavior, it's likely to affect the discipline."

6. Work together. Let them see you sweat! Choose a garden project or a job around the house that will require learning skills, patience, teamwork and persistence. You see a different side of a person when you work together.

7. Play together. Say, "After we work in the garden for two hours, we are going to take a picnic lunch to the lake and swim for four hours." Be willing to play on their turf. Do what is fun for them, even if you look goofy. This helps make you authentic!

GRACE BREEDS AUTHENTICITY

If you are looking for an example of authenticity, consider Jesus. John described him in this way: "The Word became flesh and made his dwelling among us. We have seen his glory, the glory of the One and Only, who came from the Father, full of grace and truth" (John 1:14 NIV).

Authenticity is grace and truth in relationship. It's the kind of truth seen when we are courageously honest with each other. No pretending. Nothing hidden. It's the kind of relationship that is grounded in grace. I define grace as *love in relationship:* not allowing anything to interfere with our relationship, because I love you.

It's not about being perfect—that's the law. "The law was given through Moses" (John 1:17). Jesus came to fulfill the law. The law points to our inadequacies. It sits in judgment of all humans. In contrast, Jesus came to have an authentic relationship with each of us—man, woman and child. "Grace and truth came through Jesus Christ" (John 1:17 NIV).

Remember when Jesus fed the five thousand? Mark 6:30-43 tells how the apostles were in the habit of gathering around Jesus and "reported to him all they had done and taught" (verse 30). This was their daily staff meeting, but on this particular day, they were joined by five thousand men—not to mention the women and children, who probably made up another ten thousand! Can you imagine the size of the conference table?

Authenticity is grace and truth in relationship.

That's why they met outside. But the guests were hungry. They had walked or run many miles to be with Jesus. Jesus had compassion on them and took a few loaves and fishes from a boy and miraculously fed the crowd. You probably know the story. But that wasn't the only outstanding thing that happened.

After feeding the five thousand (or fifteen thousand, depending on how you count), Jesus and his apostles pulled away into executive session. This is the remarkable part. Note that something is missing. In none of the Gospel accounts does Jesus say anything like "Okay boys, that was good today, but we can do better. Fifteen thousand is our personal record; but I think better canvassing from you, Peter, and more thorough logistics from you, Bart, and enhanced coverage by the reporters, Tom, could really take us to the next level. Oh yeah, and we need better projections and accounting, Judas." We never hear Jesus say, "Fifteen thousand is good, but next time let's push for twenty!"

To Jesus, performance wasn't as important as relationships. After the miracle, Jesus didn't push the team for "excellence" or even "working up to your potential." He didn't lead a pep rally with his disciples. Jesus sent them to their boat, while he dismissed the crowd (Matthew 14:22-23). After dismissing the crowd, "he went up on a mountainside by himself to pray." He needed to spiritually and emotionally recharge.

Then he joined his posse out on the lake. Jesus wanted to be with them, and nothing was going to interfere, not even wind, waves and water. He simply walked out on the lake and joined his crew.

Another miracle. But it wasn't simply to prove his deity; it was to be with the ones he loved.

Grace and truth in relationship.

Authentic friendship.

Kimmel captures this concept: "This kind of grace makes all the difference in the world when it's coming from God, through you, to your children. Children brought up in homes where they are free to be different, vulnerable, candid, and to make mistakes learn first-hand what the genuine love of God looks like."[2]

What would an authentic family look like? If grace and truth infiltrated all of the relationships in a family, what kind of impact would that have?

5

Learning to Listen

How was the party Saturday night?" I asked my nearly sixteen-year-old daughter Nicole on our way to school.

"Dad, it was off the hook! It was raging."

I got worried.

"There were so many people there, we couldn't believe it. When Kelsey and I drove up, there must have been fifty people on the street and in the front yard. We went inside and found another fifty around a keg of beer."

I wanted to jump in and scold, but I resisted.

"The music was too loud and we couldn't talk, so we went to the backyard. A bunch of people were back there too, all huddled around a bong." She paused and glanced at me.

My hands tightened on the steering wheel. I bit my lip and nodded.

"So we didn't want to smell like weed, so we went back into the house, but this time we went in a different sliding-glass door and we stumbled into a bedroom where this guy and some girl were having sex."

My eyes widened. The steering wheel compressed under my grip. It took great restraint, but with lips sealed I uttered, "Mmmhuh."

She took a quick glance to check my reaction, then continued, "So we decided that it wasn't the party we thought it would be and got out of there. We went to In 'n' Out and got a shake."

Thank God for In 'n' Out! "That's good, Nicole. Uh—actually, it's great! Good call."

We arrived at the school, and I kissed her goodbye.

Now I ask you, dear parent, what would have happened if I had jumped in and scolded her after "beer"?

That's right. I would have missed the "bong." (For those of you who are pretending not to know, a bong is an apparatus used to smoke marijuana.)

What would have happened if I had cut her off after "bong"?

Correct. I would have missed the "sex" part.

And what would have happened if I had interrupted her and started the interrogation after the mention of sex?

Exactly. I would have missed the part where she becomes the hero of her story.

Listening without interrupting allows our children to get themselves out of difficult situations and become the heroes of their own stories. It's not easy, and I've got the dents on the steering wheel to prove it! But it is necessary.

Now, here I just want to pause and clear the air. I want to put something in print that may not appear in other parenting books. Trust me, I've read more than a hundred of them and I haven't seen it yet. Here it goes: *Children can be mean.*

Whew! It feels good to get that off my chest. It's so refreshingly honest. In fact, let's repeat it together: Children can be mean.

You've known it, haven't you? But you probably have never said it.

It doesn't feel very "Christian" to say such things.

But it's true. At times kids are downright vicious. Let me give an example.

About two years after the beer-bong-sex escapade, I experienced déjà vu with our second daughter, Brooke. She was almost sixteen, and we were driving to school.

"How was the party on Saturday, Brooke?"

Not every moment is a teachable moment.

This time I was a little bit more prepared and didn't need to bite my lip. I'm not saying that it was easy, just that this time there was no blood. I kept my mouth shut and listened as she told a very similar story—except at the end, she and her friends went to Denny's.

Now, why do I say kids are mean? Because Nicole and Brooke had obviously spoken about the parties and traded strategies. It was the exact same scenario, except for one thing.

When I pulled up to the high school, Brooke smiled at me: "Dad, I'm proud of you."

I was taken aback. "Uh, why?"

"Because you are really learning self-control."

See what I mean? *Kids are mean!* She had been playing me like a fiddle. She was toying with me like a cat with a ball of yarn for the whole five minutes it took to get to school. Yup, kids can be mean.

But what's the real point?

Not every moment is a teachable moment. Let some go by. Your kids will give you several opportunities to interrupt them and scold or interrogate them. Refuse the temptation. It's a test! They are baiting you. They are checking to see if you really care enough to listen, just listen, without correcting, lecturing or getting the details.

GRILLED AT LUNCH

Let's say you are out to lunch with your friend. It's a sunny day, and you are enjoying the ambience of your favorite café al fresco.

"I think I'll have the cheeseburger made of Angus beef," you say.

"May I suggest the tofu salad? You look like you should lay off the beef."

You wince but decide simply to change the subject. "After lunch I want to check out the sale at the department store."

"Good idea," your friend says. "You don't look too good in those pants. They don't slenderize your figure. And by the way, don't you have a hair appointment soon? It could use some attention."

How would you feel about your friend?

I think I would move her to my *ex-friend* list, wouldn't you? Who needs the criticism and the condescension? We don't—and neither do our kids.

But we do this with our kids:

- "Sit up straight, your posture is terrible."
- "Chew with your mouth shut! What are you, an animal?"
- "You behave like monkeys. Knock it off."
- "You aren't working up to your potential."
- "I don't like your attitude."

Such comments erupting from our lips destroy communication with our kids. Constant criticism and correction interfere with communication.

I'm not saying never correct your child, just be strategic about it. Know when and where. If they are telling a story about themselves, let them finish. Resist the temptation to interrupt and instruct, because *not every moment is a teachable moment.* Let some go by.

Connect first, correct second.

LOST CONNECTION

In our society we are suffering from a huge disconnect. We spend less time with neighbors and friends than we used to. We find it challenging to maintain friendships, whether the friends are local or miles away.

Parents are disconnected from their children. We hardly have time for conversation. Instead we have a barter of data.

"When do you need to be picked up from soccer?" the mom asked her daughter via their cell phones, conveniently linked via the family plan.

"At six. Bring me a change of clothes, snack and my clarinet."

"Okay. I'll try to have dinner, probably drive-through, for you when you get home from your clarinet lesson. How did you get to soccer today?"

"Mrs. Lighetti. And it's our turn to carpool home. You have to give Jennie, Kris and Sarah a ride home. Where are you, Mom? Mom?"

"On the freeway. What time does Benji go to karate? Oops! I almost changed lanes right into a Hummer! Do you remember?"

"Remember what, Mom?"

"When does Benji have karate?"

"I dunno. Why should I know? I gotta go. Coach is here and we are supposed to be warming up, and I can't find my other shin guard. Have you seen it?"

"Seen what?"

"Never mind, Mom. See you at six."

"Wait, hold on, I have another call. It's your dad, I'll ask him."

"About my shin guards?"

"No, about Benji's karate."

Click.

Sound familiar? Most of us have days like this. How do we connect? How do we learn to listen in the midst of all the noise and activity? How will our children learn life skills and acquire personal virtues if most of our conversations are like this one?

Consider what happens if parents stay on this level and never take the time to dialogue with their children about morals and values. We need to go beyond logistics in our conversations with our kids. We need to have more than an exchange of data; we need a dialogue where each person is heard and understood.

If parents fail to pass on a sense of right and wrong, they are guilty of moral neglect.

Parents may clothe and feed their child, buy her expensive toys, sign her up for lessons and sports, but if the parents fail to pass on a sense of right and wrong, they are in fact contributing to the creation of an immoral child. We say that we are a generation that genuinely cares for its children. If that's the case, let's instill morality from the preschool years on and not back off, even during their teen years when they challenge the rules. It may be unpopular to demand certain ethical standards of our children, but it is essential.

Perhaps we need to slow down, so we have the time to listen, connect and guide. Radio talk-show host Michael Medved suggests: "If we see childhood as a time for special nurturing and exploration, we should be protecting our children from the encroachment of too many activities rather than dragging them along into our pursuit of them."[1]

A CRY TO BE HEARD

Our kids, the Millennials, are at ease growing up in the media information age. Technology is as familiar to them as their pacifiers were. Yet in the midst of this torrent of input, their voice is diminished.

Most don't feel that they "have a voice," and they want to be heard above the noise. They have high hopes for the future but feel indifferent about the present. Most would like a serious discussion with a caring adult—especially one who listens. As noted earlier, nearly all would like to have a mentor, and most would like to spend more time with their dad.[2] These kids, your kids, are eager to share their opinions and are looking for a compassionate adult to interact with. And it can be you! Unlike previous generations who dismissed their parents, not seeing them as credible sources of relevant information, today's kids are willing to give us a chance. The generation gap is dead! Our kids are crying to be listened to.

In my research with George Gallup for my book *The Seven Cries of Today's Teens,* we discovered that 91 percent of those surveyed reported a "very strong" or "strong" need to be listened to. The poll findings affirm that our teenagers and children, male and female, want their views to be considered and want to be taken seriously.[3]

Even though the survey was done with teens ages thirteen to eighteen across the United States, its findings apply for younger children as well, at least for those a few years younger, because ten-year-olds adopt the opinions, values and styles of twelve-year-olds and on down. It's safe to say our kids want to be heard.

Why?

Because when we listen to someone and really pay attention, we express value to her. This is the biblical concept of *honor.* When we listen to our child, we communicate that she has worth and is important to us. When we call someone *honorable* (as in the case of a judge), we are saying he is valuable—or originally, literally "weighty." This meaning comes from the technique of evaluating precious stones. A pound of gold is worth more than ten pounds of gravel because of its value. It's *weighty.*

If our child feels heard, she will feel honored and appreciated. When we listen, we are sharing ourselves by investing our time and attention to what she is talking about. In a media-soaked, frantic-paced world full of sound bites, it is reassuring to know that my mom or my dad will take time to listen to me.

By the way, you don't always have to have a solution. A lot of us are fix-it parents; we have solutions for everything! We have solutions for problems that our kids don't even know they have yet.

You don't always have to have a solution.

But to be a good listener we don't have to have a solution. In fact, having a solution can get in the way of effective listening. We become so preoccupied with our answer that we don't tune in to the person speaking.

A little tip that I learned, and often share with my coaching clients, is to ask, "What do you need from me?" Sometimes you can ask this before your child speaks, and he may say, "Just listen to me, Daddy." Or he may say, "Let me explain the whole deal before you start giving answers." Either way, you will have a clue regarding what your child needs. At other times, you may sense that it's best to be quiet and listen intently until your child stops; then ask, "What do you need from me?"

By the way, this is also effective in marriage! It takes much guess-work out of talking with your spouse.

Psychologist Michael Nichols says in his book *The Lost Art of Listening,*

> Listening is an art that requires openness to each other's uniqueness and tolerance of differences. The greatest threats to listening in the family are rigid roles, fixed expectations,

and pressures to conform. . . . Parents also need time alone with each of their children. One of the best ways for parents to listen to their children is to arrange little outings with each one. Once a week isn't too much to aim for. Even if a child has a good relationship with a parent, conversation and intimacy are easier away from everyday distractions. The time a parent spends taking a child out to dinner or for a hike or on a bus ride into the city may well be the best time in both of their lives.[4]

L.I.S.T.E.N.

Schedule some one-on-one time with each of your kids; try to do it weekly. Set aside twenty or thirty minutes if they are preschoolers, and thirty to forty-five minutes if they are older.

Here are six tips to keep in mind when you get together.

L — Loosen up! Try to have fun and put yourself in their sneakers. Be playful, aware that a child's economy is fun and his capital is play. You exchange value when you play with your child.

I — Invest the time. You can't hurry kids to open up and share their heart. It takes time and usually pops up sideways, when you aren't expecting it. You have to allow enough time for this to happen.

S — Stop the distractions. Put down the newspaper. Turn off the TV, computer, cell phone and PDA, and focus on your child. If you have to, go someplace where you will not be interrupted so you can talk.

T — Tune in to what your child is interested in—even if it is incredibly boring to you! Make the sacrifice for twenty minutes. Ask questions. Let her be the expert on the subject. If she has a fact wrong, you might let it go without comment just to keep things flowing.

E — Emotionally connect with your child. Try to gauge if he is happy, sad, excited, bored, worried, serene, confident or insecure. You might use a word picture to paraphrase back to him what you've heard. If you are outdoors at a park, you could say, "You look as happy as the ducks when we fed them the bread."

N — Nonverbal communication will allow you to gain additional information: pay attention to her body language, tone of voice, what is left out of the conversation and other nonverbal cues. Sometimes the nonverbal communicates more than the verbal. Don't be sidetracked by the verbal.

VENUES FOR LISTENING

Have you noticed that kids tend to open up more while you are driving in the minivan? Why is that? I think it's because they feel *even*. They feel empowered and not overwhelmed by the parent's big guns of authority and skilled adult communication. When you are riding in the car, there's a built-in distraction that actually makes conversation safer.

"Hey Mom, look—a cow!"

Which is really strange if you are driving in Manhattan!

Kids tend to open up more when we aren't looking at them eyeball to eyeball—just the opposite of adult communication.

Have you noticed that they open up more when they are busy doing something with their hands like fixing dinner, chopping vegetables or washing the dishes? Assign them chores, but be willing to sometimes do the chores with them to enable conversation.

Some good venues and activities for listening to your kids include the following:

- car trips to the country (or to the city if you live in the country)
- walks
- parks with swings and climbing sets for younger kids
- parks with grass to play catch or Frisbee for older kids
- riding bikes
- in-line skating
- a sporting event
- a museum
- walk to get ice cream or yogurt (and work off the calories)
- a zoo or animal shelter

Each morning, ask your children, "What is different about today? Anything exciting happening?" If they are having a test, game or recital, say, "I'll pray for you today."

At night, when you tuck them into bed (which you can do even in the teen years with a little persistence), ask them, "What would you like me to pray about for you?" Then pray for them. Having prayer bookend the day, morning and evening, makes the child feel heard, valued and loved.

THE BEST EXAMPLE

The best way to develop listening skills in our children is to model them ourselves. Listening is more of an art than a science, and it is best learned through modeling. As parents, we can learn from the example that God sets for us:

God's there, listening for all who pray,
     for all who pray and mean it.
He does what's best for those who fear him—

hears them call out, and saves them.

God sticks by all who love him. (Psalm 145:18-20 *The Message*)

Ready. Willing. Able. Responsive. What an example for any Christian mom or dad to aspire to!

Why should we listen to our kids and train them to listen? Because listening shows value and appreciation. Because listening opens up lines of communication to our child's heart and makes it possible to train him in other life skills and qualities. When you have developed effective listening skills, you will understand your child better, and she will understand you. You will be better equipped to be alert when something is wrong.

When we listen to our kids and let them empty themselves of negative, painful and confusing emotions, they are free to discover some positive feelings and may be more open to hearing us talk about solutions.

When we are listening instead of lecturing, we are seeking to encourage. We are looking for something to affirm that will give our child a nudge in the right direction.

Family counselors Norm Wright and Gary Oliver suggest:

What is an encouraging environment? It is one in which our kids know they are of value and worth to God and to us. It is one in which we spend more time building and encouraging them than we do scolding and correcting them. It is one in which we honor them by speaking respectfully to them. An encouraging environment is one where our emphasis is on catching them doing good rather than catching them doing bad. We invest more energy in praising them for being responsible than in criticizing and castigating them for falling short of our expectations.[5]

HELPING YOUR CHILD BE A GOOD LISTENER

1. When he wants to talk with you, ask him to come to you and not yell from another room, *"Mommy!"*

2. If your child wants to say something while you are busy talking on the phone or with another adult, she should quietly come stand next to you and touch your arm once (not incessantly). Let her know that you will pause to listen when there's a break. (Exception: if there is an emergency threatening life or limb.)

3. Insist on one person talking at a time and no interrupting. Let people finish their sentence. Also, try not to talk over each other— jumping in as the other is winding down their sentence. It's not exactly interrupting, but it's rude. (Exception: teenagers all do this when they are traveling in a herd. Let it go.)

4. Encourage responsible speech. Help your child to use his words to build others up rather than tear them down. Controlling our talk is one of the first hurdles in learning self-control. Watch out for gossip. Say to your child, "If you are not part of the problem or the solution, stay out of it, and don't talk about it." That will eliminate 80 percent of middle-schoolers' conversation topics!

5. If you have one of those chatty kids who talk too much, too long, about the same old boring (at least to you) stuff, set the egg timer for five minutes if the child is preschool age, ten minutes if she or he is older. Then say, "I will listen to you with my full attention for five minutes, then I have to . . ." This method models listening for your child, but also teaches self-editing.

6. Get rid of your stereotypes. Don't assume that what you have believed about your child is true. Don't assume that your fifth-grade daughter doesn't want to talk about boys. Don't assume that your

son doesn't want to talk about caterpillars, bugs and dinosaurs now that he is a big second-grader. Don't assume that your teen doesn't want to talk about politics, religion, finances and morality. Those were the top four most requested topics in our survey—things we never bring up as subjects at adult social functions. (Imagine it: "Hey, are you a Democrat?" "What about all of this *faith-based* bunk?" "How much do you make?" "Do you cheat on your income taxes?" It'll never happen.)

7. Indulge him with your interest, not with stuff. When a young child proudly shows his daddy his artwork from kindergarten, it's hurtful to say, "Don't brag, honey, it's not nice." Allow your child the indulgence of being your focus, your pride, the subject of your admiration for a few minutes; it won't damage him, it really won't. He'll feel loved. Allow him to showcase his accomplishments in front of those who accept him. He doesn't need achievements and material things as much as he needs your attention.

Choose one of these seven suggestions to work on with your child this week. Your simple attempts to listen will create a more encouraging environment.

We show our love best when we listen.

Are you listening?

6

Showing Empathy

I like to ask young people, "Who is cool to you?" Many times they will mention an actor, celebrity, singer or pro athlete.

Then I ask, "What happens if he is a one-hit wonder, or tears his ACL, or fades off the horizon because he flops? Would he still be cool? What happens if two years from now he is featured on VH-1's *Where Are They Now?* Would he still be cool?"

"Of course not. It wouldn't happen."

All I need to do is mention some celeb-heroes who have recently faded from the limelight, and I get their attention.

"Okay, maybe it could happen."

I encourage them: "You need to have role models beyond being cool. You can't always be cool—look at your parents." This always generates a laugh.

I'm challenging our culture's obsession with being cool. Being cool is the wrong pursuit.

The obsession to be cool is based on insecurity. It is dependent on the response of others, which is incredibly fickle and likely to change with the weather. What's cool today is not cool tomorrow. Who's hot and who's not? Being cool is being focused on self and only caring for *how I look, how I feel* and *will it be fun for me?* Chasing cool is the opposite of empathy.

I've seen a difference between students with an obsession to be cool and those with empathy. Take how a student might spend her spring break. For years I've observed this chasm between cool and the not-so-cool students. I first noticed it when I worked with teens in Newport Beach, California. Often the "cool chasers" headed to sunny places like south Florida, Cancun or a Caribbean island. Some students went with their parents to Europe for the week, while others went with their parents' credit card to Mexico for a week of parent-free frolicking. I went with a group of high school and colleges students to Mexico too— to the *deserts* of Mexico. Hot, dry, dusty, dirt-road, poverty-stricken Mexico, not an air-conditioned, pristine resort fronting the ocean.

Empathy is the ability to share in another's emotions, thoughts or feelings.

On the surface it was a split between the cool kids and those who weren't as hip or trendy. But as I looked deeper, the difference was really between those who had empathy and those who didn't.

What made the difference? What makes one young person want to drink and cavort for a week while another chooses to be thirsty, play in the dust with poor Mexican children and sleep in a grimy tent?

At some level these students realized the need in Mexico and decided that they would spend a week and try to make a difference. Did they fully understand the culture? No. Did they comprehend the sociopolitical issues? No. Were they fluent in Spanish? No. Why did they choose to serve instead of play in Mexico on their spring break?

Because they had empathy.

It's such a refreshing change from the obsession with being cool. Part of being cool in our culture is projecting a "whatever" mentality. It's common, but it is not desirable. Being tough, aloof and shielded is praised implicitly in music videos, on entertainment shows on TV, and in print and digital media. This helps explain why we follow pop-culture icons.

Donald Miller, in his provocative book *Blue Like Jazz,* muses:

> I was wondering the other day, why it is that we turn pop figures into idols? I have a theory, of course. I think we have this need to be cool, that there is this undercurrent in society that says some people are cool and some people aren't. And it is very, very important that we are cool. So, when we find somebody who is cool on television or on the radio, we associate ourselves with this person to feel valid ourselves. And the problem I have with this is that we rarely know what the person believes whom we are associating ourselves with. The problem with this is that it indicates there is less value in what people believe, what they stand for; it only matters that they are cool. In other words, who cares what I believe about life, I only care that I am cool.[1]

Being cool is a false idol. It is smoke and mirrors. It is a fruitless pursuit. Just when you figure out what is cool, or who is cool, it changes, leaving you, hopelessly, only semi-cool.

THE ACTRESS

While boarding a flight to Canada with my wife, Suzanne, I noticed a young, semi-famous actress in first class. She had on the requisite huge sunglasses, sipped her Chardonnay and thumbed through *In Style* magazine. She kept her head down, but I recognized her. I had just seen her on MTV the day before. She was rebounding from an ugly breakup, and the folks at MTV wanted everyone to know about it. Her ex was a celebrity as well, and this was, of course, "newsworthy."

We sat down and I asked Suzanne, "Did you see who was in first class?"

"No."

I mentioned the actress's name, but it didn't ring a bell. Then I immersed myself in reading a novel and forgot about her until we landed and wound up walking right behind her. She wore two-hundred-dollar jeans and four-inch heels. She appeared to be wobbly on them—probably had had two or three more Chardonnays on the flight. We went through customs and to the baggage claim area. Surprisingly, none of the young people on our flight recognized her. She didn't have an entourage, but she had an attitude—a star 'tude, as I call it. She projected *cool* by her swagger, her incessant flipping of her long blonde tresses and her compulsive yakking on her cell. I'm not sure how she did it, but she reeked entitlement. But nobody seemed to notice.

It made her mad. She wasn't getting the treatment, the attention and the props that she had come to expect in her twentysomething years on the planet.

We followed her out of baggage claim, the famous celebrity who had to roll her own Coach luggage. I found it very amusing.

A smile finally broke out when she saw a limo driver holding a tiny sign with her name on it. Only then did two teenage girls notice her and gasp. She saw them, and that was her reward. *Okay, good, I'm cool.*

If I revealed her name, you would probably not associate it with the ability to share another's feelings. She did not appear to me to be the poster child for empathy. But many girls would love to be like her.

Many guys would love to date her. She's cool.

BEYOND COOL

It's not enough to be cool or to raise cool kids. Our culture puts enough emphasis on that—we should avoid adding to it. We need to raise kids with empathy. Kids who are willing to say, "I know I'd have fun partying at spring break, but instead I'm going to build houses for the homeless in Mexico."

We need kids who challenge entitlement and develop strong empathy—the ability to *feel with* and *feel for* others, even who those are drastically different from themselves.

In North America we are suffering from a famine. This famine has nothing to do with a lack of food—most of us are overweight, and we throw away more food than some people eat. No, we have a famine of common sense. You don't have to look far to see a lack of it in public life. Just in case you don't know what I'm talking about, common sense is that skill that allows humans to make wise choices in private and public. A person with common sense is considerate of others; he thinks about their needs and preferences.

We were out to dinner this weekend with a couple we haven't seen in months. They are bright, well-read and intriguing conversationalists. I was looking forward to an engaging chat over tasty food. But a few tables over were two couples and four kids, a pile of food and not one ounce of common sense. The baby screamed at the top of her lungs, hurting my ears and interrupting our conversation. The baby's mother ignored her, which only led the one-year-old to raise the volume (which I would have thought impossible). No one at their table seemed to notice, not even the other couple. The child's screaming wasn't an expression of pain; it was frustration at not getting her way or a means of bossing her mom around and making sure she got more bread. I'm not sure. But I was sure of one thing—I had a headache!

After a few minutes, the two-year-old son of the other couple began to cry. Now we had screaming and crying going. And the four adults didn't do anything to stop it.

It was insensitive. It was unnecessary. Such displays of a lack of common sense are all too common. Just in case you are thinking, *What should they have done?* here are a few commonsense tips:

- Don't take little kids to nice restaurants.

- When you do take them out, bring snacks or crackers to feed them until their food arrives.

- Always carry a toy or crayons so they will have something to do while waiting.

- Don't allow screaming and don't reward it. Say, "If you scream, we are going to the car."

- Don't ruin someone else's conversation or dinner unless you are willing to pay for it.

- Be willing to pack up the food and leave if you can't control your kids.

Developing empathy in our kids begins with the parents being empathic—caring for the needs of others, especially in public settings. Don't expect your kids to be empathic if you haven't demonstrated concern for others when you are with your kids in public.

THE NASTY GENERATION

Child and family psychiatrist Robert Shaw reflects on the need for parents to help their children develop empathy:

> Some parents are happy that they are able to bestow on their children the freedom and possessions they themselves may have been

denied. It makes them look and feel important and loved. Doled out appropriately such "spoils" are not necessarily a bad thing. But when they become a replacement for affection or attention, perhaps offsetting parental guilt, you and your child will lose. What is the damage to a child's development for such attitudes and behaviors? The first "injury" that I see coming from manipulative spoiling is a failure to develop empathy and a lack of desire to usefully fit into situations and relationships. If a child is endlessly indulged and never hears the word "no" or experiences limits, he never has a chance to learn that other people have lives, emotions, needs, and wills of their own. Without a well-developed sense of empathy, the child will not be able to love.[2]

In their own efforts to be cool, many parents have spoiled their kids. Those parents in the restaurant wanted to look cool; they didn't want to "be the heavy" and discipline their kids. Maybe they had read an article by a guru in a magazine warning that early moral guidance is demeaning to a child and that discipline, especially in a public setting, is shaming and stunts a child's growth, expressiveness and creativity.

I'd say that guru is lacking common sense. I give much greater credence to what Shaw says: "Without a well-developed sense of empathy, the child will not be able to love."

How does a child develop empathy?

Love and limits. Children with warm, loving and firm parents develop concern for others. Children with high levels of concern for others are aware of and distressed by the fact that their inappropriate actions harm others. Children with low levels of concern (empathy) are not aware of how their misbehavior bothers others, nor do they care.

A study conducted by the National Institutes of Mental Health discovered that parenting styles significantly affect a child's development of empathy. If parents are warm and fair and set clear limits, the child develops empathy; but if parents are overly strict and harsh, or inconsistent, the child doesn't develop empathy. Appropriate guidance and limits help to teach a child how other people feel. When parents let a child run wild, they are in fact abandoning him. The study reported that infants are naturally empathic; they want to connect and feel. Injury causes a loss of empathy. A child with reduced empathy has not been given the love, bonding, guidance and nurturing she needs to thrive.[3]

> *Children with warm, loving and firm parents develop concern for others.*

I think one reason we often see a child going wild in public these days is that some of us have lost a common consensus of what is acceptable, maybe even what is "normal." Because of our obsession with being "tolerant," we have lost a shared awareness of acceptable public behavior. We are afraid to draw the line, because if we do, we will leave somebody out, and the most heinous offense in the new millennium is to exclude someone. So we put up with the screaming kids in expensive restaurants and the obnoxious behavior of middle-school students in Barnes & Noble on weekends because we feel we have to. *We gotta be cool.*

WIMPY PARENTS

But in our desire to be cool, some of us have become wimpy. We aren't just afraid *for* our kids, we are afraid *of* our kids. We wouldn't want to say anything to upset them, so we don't. The pendulum has swung too far. In the past twenty years we have improved our understanding of kids and gotten worse at setting limits for our kids. Kids used to be afraid of parents. Now parents are afraid of kids.

We encourage our kid's self-expression, but we allow him to interrupt our conversations with other adults.

We spend more time thinking about what we will buy our kid than we do thinking about why we shouldn't.

We are skilled at signing our child up for all kinds of activities, but we don't know when to say "enough."

We are skilled at signing our child up for all kinds of enrichment activities, but we don't know when to say "enough."

We are more involved with our child's sports, but we've lost precious time together as a family.

We feel compelled to meet our child's requests, but we don't take the time to separate her wants from her needs.

We want to be cool and flex our schedules and family time to accommodate our kid's hyper schedule, and we are reluctant to limit the kid's schedule for the benefit of the family.

We have come a long way in learning how to nurture children, but not as far when it comes to nurturing our marriage. We haven't learned to protect our marriage from the demands of our kids.

We have it backwards. We have become wimpy.

I struggle with this too. I'm so disappointed in myself when I give in to the selfish demands of my child. "Why do I do this?"

I think it has to do with a warped view of our kids. We see them as customers, and "the customer is always right." In a way we have become servants to our kids. William Doherty's words about this are like a glass of ice water in the face:

In the new culture of childhood, children are viewed as *consumers* of parental services, and parents are viewed as *providers* of parental services and *brokers* of community services for children. What gets lost is the other side of the human equation: children bearing responsibilities to their family and communities. In a balanced world, children are expected not only to receive from adults but also to actively contribute to the world around them, to help care for the younger and the infirm, to add their own marks to the quality of family life, and to contribute to the common good in their school and communities. If children live only as consumers of parental and community services, then they are not active citizens of families and communities.[4]

For our kids to develop empathy, we need to help them discover that it's *not about them*. We aren't here to provide services to them. A parent is not his child's concierge. We are a family, not a market economy. We don't have to provide the newest, best, most convenient, hippest service for our child. We need to be willing to displease the "customer" for her own benefit. When we serve our kids too much, we create an overblown sense of entitlement and destroy empathy in them, and we become insecure as parents.

Helping kids develop empathy begins with simple things—mostly things they do not want to do:

- clean up their toys
- wash their hands before a meal
- come to dinner on time
- show manners at the table
- participate in polite conversation during the meal
- listen without interrupting

- help clean up after the meal
- willingly do their chores
- go to bed on time without a fuss

When we require our kids to do these kinds of things, it helps them become secure in the family. They become contributing parts of the team, not demanding consumers. It helps them feel valued, and it teaches them to be other-centered. It requires them to consider the feelings of others. It calls for suspending "what I want" at this moment to consider what others need. It helps them develop empathy.

It is difficult to develop empathy in our culture because so much works against it. The opposite of empathy is narcissism, and it has a huge fan club. It's like that old yarn, "Enough about me. Let's talk about you. What do you think about me?"

ISAAC THE WATER CARRIER

An old Yiddish folk story tells of a well-to-do gentleman who had a passion for the Hebrew Scriptures. He went to a wise old rabbi and posed a concern: "I think I grasp the sense and meaning of these writings except for one thing. I cannot understand how we can be expected to give God thanks for our troubles."

The rabbi knew instantly that he could not explain this with mere words. He said to the gentleman: "If you want to understand this, you will have to visit Isaac the water carrier."

The gentleman was mystified by this, but knowing the rabbi to be wise, he crossed to a poor section of the settlement and came upon Isaac the water carrier, an old man who had been engaged in mean, lowly, backbreaking labor for over fifty years. He explained the reason for his visit.

Isaac paused from his labors. Finally, after several minutes of silence, looking baffled, he spoke: "I know that the rabbi is the wisest of men. But I cannot understand why he would send you to me with that question. I can't answer it because I've had nothing but wonderful things happen to me. I thank God every morning and night for all his many blessings on me and my family."

Perspective.

Isaac had the right perspective; as a result he was a joyous, empathic man. In many ways he was very wealthy.

EMPATHY EXERCISES

Developing genuine empathy in your child means going the second mile. It means bypassing the easiest route. Empathy at its root is love expressed in action.

> Pure and lasting religion in the sight of God our Father means that we must care for orphans and widows in their troubles, and refuse to let the world corrupt us. . . .
>
> Dear brothers and sisters, what's the use of saying you have faith if you don't prove it by your actions? That kind of faith can't save anyone. Suppose you see a brother or sister who needs food or clothing, and you say, "Well, good-bye and God bless you; stay warm and eat well"—but then you don't give that person any food or clothing. What good does that do?
>
> So you see, it isn't enough just to have faith. Faith that doesn't show itself by good deeds is no faith at all—it is dead and useless. (James 1:27; 2:14-17 NLT)

A busy schedule of enrichment activities won't develop genuine empathy in your child; but giving up some of your grocery budget to feed, clothe, house and educate an orphan will. Imagine sitting down to a family dinner of soup. You say, "We are going to have soup once a week. With the money we save, we are going to sponsor a child through Compassion International. We will pray for him, write him and sacrifice some of our grocery money for him. Here is a picture of him. His name is Javier, and he lives in a very poor section of a huge city in Venezuela."

We need to go beyond the fake and temporary issues that would divert us to the externals, and move to develop genuine sacrifice and empathy—from the inside out.

SCOTT'S EPIPHANY

Scott is a typical fifteen-year-old. He's into basketball, girls, surfing and video games. He's not into school. His parents are—they are both teachers. They were concerned with his grades and attitude, so they brought him to me, the family coach.

"So school isn't that important to you?"

"Nah, but I have to go so I can play sports. I do like to hang out with my friends at lunch and meet girls, so it's not all bad."

"What is going on with your parents and school?"

"They think I can do better. They are disappointed with my grades. Grades are a *huge* deal to them."

"It's their world, you know."

"Yeah."

"Are they expecting too much?"

"Yeah. They want me to get A's. I've never gotten A's."

"What are you getting now?"

"C's and a few D's." Sitting cross-legged, he looked down at the sneaker on his knee and played with the laces.

"Can you do better?"

"Yeah."

"What do you need to do better?"

"I dunno."

"Could you use a tutor for English?"

"Yeah."

"What about math?"

"I'm okay there; it's my best subject. I just have to do the work."

"All right. Let's say you do the work for math, get a tutor for English and put in an hour every day on homework, even if you don't think you have any. What do you need to raise your Spanish grade?"

"A reason."

"Isn't your youth group going to Mexico over spring break?"

"Yeah, I went last year. It was cool. But I was going to hang out with my friends and hit the beach and shoot hoops."

"Did you meet some kids last year in Mexico?"

"Yeah, and I couldn't talk with them, other than 'hola.'"

"Could you use your Spanish now? Would it be fun to go back and actually talk with your friends?"

His face lit up. "Yeah, that would be cool. I'd like to see some of them. I think I could actually talk with them now."

"Well, there's your reason. Use Spanish to prepare you to talk with those kids. Focus on learning the vocabulary to talk with them, to see them get excited talking with you. Don't worry about the grade."

"All right." He smiled.

I talked with his parents and asked them to lower their expectations for grades but raise their expectations for and involvement in helping Scott focus on others. They agreed and were surprised at the change in his attitude and demeanor at home. He became less argumentative and moody and more cooperative, and he managed to raise his grades in all of his classes. He spent a month getting ready to go to Mexico on spring break. He learned to concern himself with the needs and feelings of others. He learned empathy.

7

Demonstrating Compassion

This certainly is better than the dried crust of bread and one-onion soup we had in Ravensbruck," said the seventysomething woman as she ladled a large serving of my mother's garlic mashed potatoes onto her plate.

"What is one-onion soup?" I asked.

"They would prepare a big pot of soup and use only water and one onion, sometimes throwing in some garbage for flavor, and they called it 'soup.'" She smiled, and her cheeks reminded me of fresh, hot rolls. There were hardly any lines around her eyes. For a woman who had survived the Holocaust, her sense of humor surprised me.

"Now Timmy, tell me about what you like to do. I hear you play soccer."

"Yes, I'm playing for my third year now. I play goalie."

"I love football, or 'soccer' as you Americans say. Willem, my brother, played in Holland. He was quite good. But that was before . . ." Her voice trailed off.

When I was growing up, we had lots of dinner guests, but this time the guest was interesting. Sitting at our dining-room table was

Corrie ten Boom, the concentration camp survivor, author of the bestselling *The Hiding Place* and compassionate resistance leader who saved Jews from capture by the Nazis in Holland. She was in town for a speaking engagement, and it was our privilege to have her in our home. She came to our house a couple times, and each time she regaled us with exciting tales. It was better than TV.

The ten Booms were devoted Christians who dedicated their lives to service to their fellow human beings. Their home was open to anyone in need. Through the decades they were very active in social work in Haarlem, the Netherlands, and their faith inspired them to serve their Christian brothers and sisters and society at large.

During World War II, the ten Boom home became a refuge, a hiding place, for fugitives and those hunted by the Nazis. Their vibrant faith led them to hide Jews, students who refused to cooperate with the Nazis, and members of the Dutch underground resistance movement. There were usually six or seven people illegally living in their home. Through these activities the ten Boom family and their many friends saved the lives of nearly one thousand Jews.

On February 28, 1944, the ten Boom family was betrayed, and the Gestapo (the Nazi secret police) raided their home. The Gestapo set a trap and waited throughout the day, seizing everyone who came to the house.

Because of their compassion, four ten Booms lost their lives in the concentration camps. Corrie, however, came home from the death camp. She realized her life was a gift from God and she needed to share what she and her sister Betsy had learned in Ravensbruck: "There is no pit so deep that God's love is not deeper still," and "God will give us the love to be able to forgive our enemies."[1]

As Corrie talked about her experiences, I remained quiet as long as I could, then burst out, "So how did people contact you? Did you have a secret code or something?" I was a fan of secret agent movies and TV shows, like *The Man from U.N.C.L.E.*

"Yes," Corrie smiled and rubbed the top of my head, "we had codes. Our house was above my papa's watch shop, and I worked there. In fact, I was the first woman to be a certified watchmaker in all of Holland. I thought I would be fixing watches all my life, but God had other plans. *His* time." She paused to see if I got the pun. "If someone wanted help, they would ask, 'We have an old watch with an unusual face. Do you know someone who would like to buy it?'"

"What did that mean?"

"It meant that they had an elderly Jew whom they wanted to help hide from the Nazis."

"That's neat. Weren't you scared? I mean, in some movies I've seen how angry the Nazis could get."

"Yes, we were all afraid; those were frightening times. But as I like to say, there is no pit so deep that God's love is not deeper still." She turned to eat her chicken.

What kind of pit is she talking about? I mused. Being eleven, I still thought in concrete terms most of the time. I didn't realize that she was speaking metaphorically. I thought of some deep, dark, hellish hole filled with Nazis. *How could God's love go there? I mean, why bother? Why not let them fry in hell? She must not mean that God's love reaches out to real losers like Nazis!* "How could you handle it? The SS had to be watching you and the watch shop."

"Yes, they were. But I learned God's Word, and it served me well. When I was afraid I would think about it. 'You are my refuge and my shield; your word is my only source of hope.' Psalm 119. And later, 'Don't leave me to the mercy of my enemies, for I have done what is just and right.'"

I was impressed with Corrie's ability to quote Scripture, tell intriguing stories and still get down on the floor and play with us. We played Monopoly on the living-room floor. She laughed boisterously when she got a "Go to Jail" card: "It's not like I haven't been there before!" She tussled my hair and listened to me with her eyes. She reminded me of Jesus.

GROWING COMPASSIONATE KIDS

I can't even begin to grasp Corrie ten Boom's compassion for the oppressed Jews in her home country. She risked her life to rescue them. She didn't try to convert them to Christianity first; she simply lived out her faith in front of them. Her deep faith prompted compassion. There is a profound link between conviction, compassion and courage.

Growing compassion in the lives of our children is difficult because there are so many forces that oppose it.

Growing compassion in the lives of our children is difficult because there are so many forces that oppose it. But our kids can learn to be caring and compassionate at home. Corrie did. And her compassion meant life for hundreds.

Doug Huneke, a pastor and religious educator, wanted to understand what makes people compassionate. He interviewed three hundred rescuers of Jews during the Holocaust. He wanted to discover why some people helped while others passively stood by. What made the heroes risk their lives to help others? He discovered four qualities and six experiences they had in common. These ten characteristics are explored in detail in his book *The Moses of Rovno,* which tells the story of one exceptional rescuer named Fritz Graebe.[2]

Qualities of a hero

- adventuresomeness
- ability to speak up
- ability to examine prejudices
- empathic imagination (imagining the effect of a negative situation on a person)

Experiences of a hero

- being marginalized, left out or undervalued
- being exposed to suffering at an early age
- cooperating to promote the well-being of others
- having a morally strong parent with whom you felt close
- living in a home where hospitality was highly valued
- belonging to a group that values compassion

What a wonderful list for parents to consider! Just think of all the applications: Your son likes to go on hikes and often gets lost exploring. Don't sweat it; he is an adventurer! He may have the right stuff for a hero.

Your daughter is always giving you lip and won't back down in an argument. You are sure she could be a lawyer, even though she's only twelve. Don't fret; her insistence on having her say can be used to speak up for the oppressed.

Your son accuses you of racism when you make a brief, insignificant comment about someone of a different race. His ability to detect prejudice can be directed to challenge discrimination and injustice.

Your daughter seems "too sensitive" to you because she can imagine the effect of harmful situations on others. But this same sensitivity can motivate her to relieve suffering.

Your child feels left out because she doesn't make a sports team. This experience of rejection may just be what she needs to rally compassion for the undervalued.

Your son has to be hospitalized as a five-year-old. His exposure to suffering could make him sensitive to others with health concerns and disabilities.

You daughter learns to cooperate with team members and wins a soccer championship. Her positive experience leads her to seek out other collaborative efforts that benefit others.

Your strong morals and bonding with your son help him feel secure and empowered to do what is right because he can picture you doing it.

Your home is a place of laughter, hospitality and warmth, especially for people who are different from you. Your family hosts a small group that plans family service projects that benefit the homeless and needy in your community.

See how these experiences and characteristics add up to creating a compassionate child? A lot depends on one's perspective. An experience may be negative for your child, but with a bit of alert parenting, you can turn it into a learning experience that generates compassion. Pain often generates compassion. Don't isolate your child from all pain. If you do, you are making him weak and uncaring.

You may have been focused on getting your child admitted to the right private school or helping him make a traveling team in a sport or become proficient at a musical instrument. These goals are commendable, but they may not make your child more caring and compassionate. The irony is that being turned down by the school, being rejected by the team's coach and not making first chair in clarinet may actually be very helpful for the development of your child's character. And that, ten years from now, may be important than the other things anyway.

WHY WE DON'T TEACH OUR KIDS COMPASSION

"I'm not going to allow my daughter to go with you to Mexico again!" exclaimed the father. Already his temples were turning pink. "She's turning into some kind of bleeding-heart liberal. All she wants to do is serve the poor now."

"I'm sorry you feel that way. Our goal was to expose her to need in the world, not isolate her from it. The need will still be there even if she doesn't go with us next year. I think being in Mexico made her feel important because she was needed and could contribute."

"That's not important to me. She needs to focus on her grades, her debutante ball and her tennis if she wants to make it into USC."

"We are trying to help kids develop compassion, not simply socialize them into nice citizens."

"Not with my daughter!" he stormed off. And he was a member of our church!

So why is it that some of us parents, like this frustrated dad, don't teach our kids compassion?

It's depressing. What can one family do? It's discouraging and overwhelming trying to teach our kids about the world's huge needs.

It's political. We don't want to get involved in a "red" versus "blue" partisan debate.

It's not our world. We stay away from neighborhoods like that—too seedy and dangerous for my kids.

It's not our job. Why can't the church teach this kind of stuff, not the family? Or maybe the school should—in a civics class or something. Does it really fall to us—the parents?

We don't want to scare our child. Why should she have to think about those terrible things? She's just a kid.

It will be uncomfortable for my child and me. We have worked hard to get to a place that is easy; I don't want to mess that up.

We are too busy to bother ourselves with other people's issues. Aren't there government agencies that take care of these kinds of thing? We don't have the time to bother with them.

I really don't care about the problems of those people. I don't know them, and don't want to, and really don't want to concern myself with their troubles.

These reasons that we don't teach our kids compassion are very common. But they are not biblical. In fact, they are counter to the Word of God and the heart of God.

WHY WE SHOULD TEACH OUR KIDS COMPASSION

Jan Johnson says it best in her excellent book *Growing Compassionate Kids:*

> Over the years, I've continually gotten bogged down with the minutiae of parenting and let the compassionate emphasis slide. The one thing that brings me back to it over and over is reading and hearing the Gospels. In the Gospel narratives, I'm constantly fascinated and challenged by Jesus, who proclaimed truth about himself while offering cups of cold water to throwaways. He crossed barriers without a second thought, seeing only the heart of the person in front of him. He was of one heart with God, the protector of these throwaways. Each time I encounter Christ's radical behavior, I walk away wanting to behave as he did.[3]

Like Johnson, I'm always amazed at Jesus. He doesn't follow the advice of contemporary public relations experts or the branding specialists. Instead of associating himself with the winners, he spends time with the losers. He reflects the heart of his Father.

Jesus showed mercy to the poor. He considered their needs.

The Spirit of the Lord is upon me,
    for he has appointed me to preach Good News to the poor.
He has sent me to proclaim
    that captives will be released,
    that the blind will see,
    that the downtrodden will be freed from their oppressors,
    and that the time of the Lord's favor has come. (Luke 4:18-19 NLT)

Do we know and care about the downtrodden? About half of the world's population is so poor that they don't have enough to eat. Some live in your community.

Jesus called attention to the throwaways—those who had been marginalized.

Then those "sheep" are going to say, "Master, what are you talking about? When did we ever see you hungry and feed you, thirsty and give you a drink? And when did we ever see you sick or in prison and come to you?" Then the King will say, "I'm telling the solemn truth: Whenever you did one of these things to someone overlooked or ignored, that was me—you did it to me."

Then he will turn to the "goats," the ones on his left, and say, "Get out, worthless goats! You're good for nothing but the fires of hell. And why? Because—

I was hungry and you gave me no meal.
I was thirsty and you gave me no drink.

I was homeless and you gave me no bed.

I was shivering and you gave me no clothes,

Sick and in prison, and you never visited." (Matthew 25:37-
43 *The Message*)

Jesus had compassion on others as well:

- The poor and shivering—those without proper warm clothing due to poverty. Idea: Could you start in your closet and give away clothes you haven't worn lately?

- The sick. There are children (as well as adults) with incurable diseases in every community. Idea: What could your family do to encourage them? How could you show compassion to HIV/ AIDs patients?

- Those who were in prison. My heart breaks for kids in juvenile facilities and for kids who have an incarcerated parent. Ask yourself, *Should I be involved?* Idea: What about writing to in- mates or supporting ministries like Prison Fellowship? Or pro- viding Christmas gifts, camping or mentoring for children of inmates? Check out www.projectangeltree.org .

- Strangers. The economics of our time have caused millions of people to move to urban centers—some from other countries, some from other states. All of them feel like strangers. Idea: Dis- cuss together, "What can we do as a family to welcome strang- ers?" Start with the new kid at school or the new family in your neighborhood.

We need to combine our compassion with courage if we are go- ing to reflect the heart of God, because he seeks justice for the op- pressed:

Give fair judgment to the poor and the orphan;

uphold the rights of the oppressed and the destitute.
Rescue the poor and helpless;

> deliver them from the grasp of evil people. (Psalm 82:3-4
> NLT)

So our task goes beyond raising nice kids; it's helping our kids demonstrate compassion by standing *for* something and demonstrate courage by standing *against* something.

> ## *Our task goes beyond raising nice kids; it's helping our kids demonstrate compassion by standing* for *something and demonstrate courage by standing against something.*

How to Grow Compassion in Your Kids

1. Model caring values. Demonstrate caring in front of your kids.

2. Provide opportunities to demonstrate compassion. Once a month, plan an activity for you and your children to do together to practice compassion.

3. Model compassion in the discipline of your child. Our kids can give us plenty of reasons to be angry with them, but when we stop and don't react in anger, we are demonstrating grace to them. Our kids will learn from this. They will see how we suspend our anger and imagine how the other person feels.

4. Show compassion through the care of pets and the garden. Even little children can learn kindness and caring by taking care of their pet or tending a garden. Compassion means seeing life from a

puppy's point of view, even though she just chewed up your shoes!

5. Get your children involved in care for extended family members—Grandma or Grandpa, or "adopted" grandparents. Older people have needs that kids can meet. This helps both feel valued, included and loved.

6. Teach your child to be reflective. Ask her questions about persons in situations that call for our compassion: poverty, exploitation, natural disasters, war and famine. To bring it closer to home, you could ask, "How does it feel to be the new kid at a school?"

7. Make it personal. Try to link a situation with a real person. For example, by "adopting" a child through Compassion International and praying for him at meals, you can make a connection between a global circumstance (widespread poverty and hunger) and an actual person. (See www.compassion.com.) If someone makes a blanket accusation against a certain racial group, balance that with "Our neighbors are of that race and they are not anything like that, are they?"

8. Demonstrate hospitality on a regular basis. When we model hospitality we are showing value by creating room in our busy lives for strangers and friends. We sacrifice time, money and comfort to show them hospitality.

MEET YOUR NEIGHBOR

"Who is my neighbor?" you may be asking, echoing the expert in the Jewish law (Luke 10:29). Who should be the recipients of our compassion?

If we follow Jesus' lead, we'll make these decisions based on "upside-down" values. Instead of admiring the rich and famous, we call attention to the poor and forgotten. Instead of emulating the powerful, we seek to empower the oppressed. Instead of chasing after the strong—celebrated athletes, for example—we give significant time, money and attention to the weak and the sick. The kingdom of God turns our world's values upside down.

Jan Johnson explains:

Every society has its hierarchy of worthiness. Voiceless people include anyone lower on the cultural ladder than others. They must keep quiet because of their power-down positions in society. Some power-down/power-up relationships we recognize are

- Children as opposed to adults
- Women as opposed to men
- Minority races as opposed to majority races
- Poor as opposed to middle class; middle class as opposed to rich
- Lower-paid workers as opposed to highly paid workers
- Less intelligent as opposed to the more intelligent
- Labor as opposed to management
- Blue-collar workers as opposed to professionals

When voiceless people do speak up, no one takes them seriously because they don't have the status, money, age, or know-how to command respect. Jesus, however, routinely put ordinary, voiceless people in power-up positions.[4]

When we show compassion to the least of these and teach our kids to be compassionate toward those without a voice, we are being the hands and feet of Christ.

8

Developing Discernment

T ony is leading our small group, but people are quitting left and right. I'm not sure what it is, but something's going on," exclaimed Roberto.

"Like what?" I asked.

"It's eerie. There's a dark presence in Shari's living room where we meet, but it only seems to be there when Tony is there. I've been at Shari's before we started the group, and I didn't sense it then."

"Are people getting into the Bible study and praying for each other?"

"No, not as much as we used to. Lately we've been arguing more about petty issues, and people are getting hurt. It just seems like we're on edge."

I took a deep breath and quickly prayed silently. As a pastor, I had inherited oversight of this new group as part of my expanded shepherding responsibilities. "Has any pastor met with Tony?"

"Nah, I just think he went to the training, filled out the paperwork and started leading. Nobody seems to have known him before this group started. It's like he didn't exist until three months ago."

"Uh-huh. Do we know anything about his personal life?"

"Yeah, he is into some things that don't add up. I'm not really up on everything, but I sense something is off with him and I think it's agitating the group. Like last night we got into a big argument about Jesus being the only way of salvation. Tony was actually challenging that. And he's the leader!"

"What does he say?"

"He thinks it's too rigid. He believes God has 'multiple channels for his grace and power,' is how he puts it. Two weeks ago somebody brought up a prayer concern about their teenager getting into Wicca, and he interrupted them to defend it."

"I'll meet with him, Roberto. Thanks for your call."

Later that week I met with Tony. He wore black cowboy boots, black jeans and a black long-sleeved shirt with the top three buttons unbuttoned, exposing his ample chest hair. His raven-colored hair was gelled straight back, and he offered a gleaming white smile as he pumped my hand. "How ya doin'? Nice to meet ya. I've seen ya around but didn't meet ya yet."

I felt like I was meeting one of the Sopranos who had gotten displaced in Texas. "Nice to meet you, Tony. I want to get to know all of the small group leaders, and I hadn't met you yet. Tell me about yourself."

He said a few things about his background, but it was quite vague.

"Tony, do you believe that Jesus is the only way for salvation? Do you believe that he paid the price on the cross for you and was resurrected to demonstrate his power as God?"

He shifted in his seat, looked up at the ceiling, "No, I really don't believe it like you do. God is not that uptight."

"What do you mean?"

"He can use Hinduism, Islam, Wicca and your old-school Christianity to get people to him. Same god, many paths." He reached to adjust his pants cuff over his silver-tipped boot. As he bent over, a gold chain with a pentagram swung loose from underneath his shirt.

"Why do you wear a pentagram?"

"I believe in its power. We can have more power if we want."

"You're not talking about power in Jesus, are you?"

His eyes barreled into mine. The friendly New Jersey persona disappeared, and a cold, calculating gray shone in his eyes. "No, he's overrated."

"You are leading this group with the powers of darkness, aren't you?"

A sinister smile came to his lips. "Yes, yes I am. Is that a problem?"

"We are a Christian church which believes that Jesus is God's Son and he has provided the only way for us to experience God's grace and forgiveness—everything else is a decoy. You are deceiving people, and I don't want you leading the small group anymore."

"All right, no big deal. There's plenty of fish in the sea. They were a bunch of nerdy Bible kissers anyway."

"You are practicing now, aren't you?"

He raised his eyebrows and chuckled. "Yeah, I'm a warlock—have been for years. We have a coven right here in town." He smirked. "I guess the jig is up."

"Yeah, it is."

Tony was an active, practicing Wiccan warlock with a position of leadership in our church! He had deceived the leaders and slipped under the radar with the intent of covertly leading the faithful astray.

Thankfully, the application of a bit of discernment helped reveal what was going on. Roberto and I had been able to see something that others had missed—that Tony was working against us, not for us.

I know this story doesn't come from the world of family life, but it dramatically illustrates what can happen when discernment is lacking. The stakes are just as high at home as they are in the church—maybe higher.

As parents, we need discernment. Our kids need discernment. Discernment allows us to quickly assess a person's motives and perceive if he is for us or against us. We live in a post-innocence culture that requires us to be alert and discerning. We can't take each person at face value. We have to look deeper. We have to discern.

Discernment—we all want it for our children. What is it?

I like to define discernment as *the ability to make wise choices under pressure.* Discernment means demonstrating sensible judgment or understanding. It is the insight that highlights differences. It is heightened mental contrast. It is the perception that goes deep under the surface to discover and reveal the true nature of a thing or a person.

> *We live in a post-innocence culture that requires us to be alert and discerning.*

As parents, we need discernment in many situations—for example, to

- know if a childcare provider is safe for our infant
- judge if a particular preschool is best for our child
- know if our child is ready for kindergarten
- recognize that certain children don't make good playmates for our kids
- know if our child should be educated in home school, private school or public school
- sense when we have our child involved in too many activities
- be alert to negative influences of media and peers on our children

Our kids need discernment too, if they are going to successfully navigate their world. They can learn it from us if we are available, but if we are not, they will learn something else. Richard Louv, author of *Childhood's Future,* warns: "To whom do children turn when their parents do not have enough time for them? To other time givers, some benign, some not so benign. To peers, to gangs, to early sex partners, to the new electronic bubble of computers and video."[1]

Simply put, you need to train your children to make wise decisions and use discernment, or they will be swayed by the predominant wave of the culture, which is most likely to be hedonism. Instead of making decisions from a framework of values and principles, they will be making decisions based on what brings pleasure, what is fun or what's-in-it-for-me. If you don't want your children living with a beer commercial mentality, then you need to train them to have discernment—to make wise decisions based on timeless principles. To not do so is to turn them over to the prevailing winds of the world's values.

Researcher George Barna reminds us that children matter on the battlefront:

If we do a great job of training children to love God with all their heart, mind, strength and soul, then we will no longer have to invest time battling over moral and spiritual issues such as abortion, homosexuality, gambling and pornography. . . . If we effectively teach God's principles and expectations to our youngsters and instill within them a thirst for righteousness and a passion for God, the need to wage a culture war will be eliminated by reshaping the culture from within. The cumulative effect of their character and beliefs will redefine the contours of the culture.[2]

PROTECT VERSUS PREPARE

I often am sucked into the school debate: Public school or Christian school? Home school or Christian school? Home school or public school? In some cases, though, the school doesn't matter. What matters is how the parents perceive their role. In most families, this is actually more important than the school where the child spends six hours a day. What is going on in the life of the child for the other eighteen hours?

Some parents feel it is their job to isolate their children from the evils of the culture and the pains of the world. This viewpoint often shapes their school decisions when kindergarten approaches.

Indeed it is important to protect our children, especially when they are young, but as they mature, we do well to change our focus from protection to preparation. We want to train them to be ready, to be prepared to take on life's challenges.

I probably advocate this philosophy because I was in Boy Scouts for years and our motto was "Be prepared." It's a good motto for boys *and* for girls. If we are prepared for challenges and choices, the odds of our making wise decisions will be much higher. It's when we aren't prepared that we make foolish and dangerous choices. I have seen many parents focus solely on the protection side of the equation to the neglect of the preparation side and wind up with a disaster.

You can foster a preparation mentality beginning when your children are quite young. With a three-year-old you might say, "It's good to learn how to eat your lunch, take a nap and wash your hands after using the bathroom because this is what the big kids do at preschool. If you want to go to preschool, you have to do these three things."

The idea is to *help your child do more as you do less.* You are in a countdown to independence. When your child is born, you have 100 percent responsibility for her, but as she matures, you give her more freedom and more responsibility to make choices. You say, in effect, "I want to work myself out of a job—the job of controlling you and making decisions for you. I want to give you more freedom as you assume more responsibility. Are you interested?"

Help your child do more as you do less.

Your child will jump at the chance. Why? Because you are giving her what she wants—freedom and autonomy. But before you let the reins out too far, you have to know that she will make wise choices when she is away from you. Figure 1 provides a graphic representation that may be helpful.

Help Your Kids Do More As You Do Less

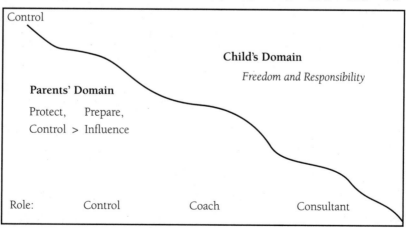

Figure 1. Countdown to independence

Use figure 1 to prepare your child for independence (you'll find a version suitable for photocopying in appendix three). Say, "When you were a baby, we had 100 percent responsibility for you. We had to carry you everywhere, feed you, change you and not leave you alone. But as you got older, you could do these things for yourself—thankfully! Now we want to keep it up by giving you more freedom and responsibility. We want to give you more choices. You will need to learn how to make wise choices because you will have to deal with the results, good or bad."

At each birthday turn over one more choice to your child. Make a formal presentation in writing: "Now that you are thirteen, you have all of the rights, privileges and responsibilities of a thirteen-year-old. You can now go to PG-13 movies. Choose wisely, knowing what's important to our family."

See how this works? You are helping your child do more as you do less. In this setup our kids have to think. This is what helps them learn discernment.

REMOTE-CONTROL PARENTING

Wouldn't be great if we had a remote for our kids?

Stop:	The kid freezes.
Mute:	The kid goes silent.
Change:	The kid changes his attitude or topic of conversation.
Pause:	"I don't want to deal with this now, so . . ." Pause.
Sleep:	Point it to yourself to grab a nap, or at your kid.
Rewind:	"Oops! I didn't mean to say that." Do-over.
Play:	Everyone laughs and plays together.
Fast Forward:	I don't like the teen years. I'm going to FFWD.
Menu:	The kid cheerfully fixes our favorite meal and serves us.

If only technology could catch up to the market! We'd all buy one, wouldn't we?

There is a way to "control" our kids at a distance, and it doesn't involve shocking collars like they use on dogs, night vision goggles, or reward pellets like they use with pigeons. Here's how to influence your child from a distance:

1. Define your expectations. Put them in writing.

2. Decide on consequences if the expectations are not met. Put these in writing.

3. Inform your child of the expectation and the consequences (both positive and negative). Remind your child that it is *their* choice. Your role will be to apply the consequences. They will know in advance, so there's no need for whining, cajoling or throwing temper tantrums—especially if your child is fifteen or older!

4. Refer to the agreement and reinforce it as needed. (Make back-up copies.) When they misbehave, ask, "What does our agreement say?"

"I dunno," she says, looking at the carpet.

"Go get your copy."

"I lost it."

"Okay, I happen to have another copy here. It says, 'If I don't put my bike away by sunset, I don't get to ride it for three days. If I put my bike away every night by sunset, I get to ride it.' Go put your bike in the garage, and I'll be out to lock it up in a few minutes."

See how you do it? No stress. No yelling. No fretting over the discipline. You are helping prepare your child by making her be responsible for *her* decisions. This is the way she learns to be discerning and make wise decisions when she is away from you. This is remote-control parenting. (See the Consequences Worksheet in appendix four.)

Remote-control parenting means moving from a position of control to a position of influence. We really can't control our kids anyway. As soon as they go off to school, or Sunday school, we can't monitor everything that happens. But we can influence them at a distance. We can help them integrate values and make choices based on consequences. When we do this, we are growing discernment in our child.

If we don't gradually prepare our kids to live in the hostile environment of our age, the wolves of the world, the flesh and the devil will devour them. And at times, it looks like our kids are already being devoured by the enemy. I know parents who have maintained their kids in safe, sterilized Christian "incubators" through their entire childhood, only to be stunned by their active or passive rejecting of Christian values when they become teens.

We need to prepare our kids from the inside out and then send them to be tested.

It's not enough to protect our kids from the outside; we need to prepare them from the inside out and then send them to be tested. I know this sounds risky, but we are to be "salt and light" to a tasteless and dark world. Jesus said it first: "Let me tell you why you are here. You're here to be salt-seasoning that brings out the God-flavors of this earth. If you lose your saltiness, how will people taste godliness? You've lost your usefulness and will end up in the garbage" (Matthew 5:13 *The Message*). If we keep ourselves—and our children—comfy and cozy in the saltshaker, what good is that?

It seems to me that some Christian parents are wrapped up in creating their children to be exquisite saltshakers. They are made of fine crystal, with silver tops and perfectly engineered pour holes; but the salt stays in the shaker and it has gone flat.

I talk with nonchurch people every week. Their view of most Christians? That they have "lost their usefulness." "They aren't relevant." We need to do a better job of being salt. We need to do a better job of helping our kids be salt and bring out the God-flavors of this earth. Being an effective Christian parent means *spicing it up*.

Tim Kimmel warns us not to wrap ourselves up in bland "cocoon Christianity":

> Parents whose goal is to raise a spiritually safe kid usually get a spiritually safe kid in the process. But they also often get a spiritually *weak* kid. The child is weak when it comes to standing up against the harsh pressures of a lost world. Once they are exposed to the full gale, down they go. On the other hand, parents who want to raise strong children realize it cannot happen without the children having to work their spiritual muscles. They realize that no cultural pain results in no spiritual gain.[3]

INSIDE GAME

I love the March Madness of college basketball. You never know what is going to happen when you have skilled adolescents on the court! We like watching both the women and the men. We especially appreciate a team that has an inside game—one that can play in the paint, up close to the hoop, by either shooting or passing out—and an outside game, away from the basket, spreading across the court and setting up long-range shots with picks and passes to the paint with cutters. A great team will have an inside game and an outside game *and* will be excellent defenders.

Good parents are the same: they have an inside game and an outside game and are excellent defenders.

Suzanne and I decided that we wanted to work on our "inside

game" as parents when our daughters were very young. We wanted them to have certain character qualities, skills and experiences that would serve them well as they got older. Suzanne was a social worker and I was a youth worker, so we knew the trouble that kids and families can get into. We decided that the best approach was not to isolate our kids in a monastery but to prepare them to go out into the world with strength from within. We enrolled them in public school. It seemed right for us. I know not everyone agrees, but it worked for us.

But we knew that we had to develop discernment with our kids as we sent them off to school. The "inside game" is a combination of discernment and the heart. We weren't too worried about the pluralistic worldview, evolution or antifaith sentiments; we knew we could

The battle for our kids is not for their heads—it is for their hearts.

deal with those at home, through discussions after school, at the dinner table and as we helped with homework. We were concerned with their hearts. The battle for our kids is not for their heads—it is for their hearts.

The prophet Jeremiah highlights this: "The human heart is most deceitful and desperately wicked. Who really knows how bad it is? But I know! I, the LORD, search all hearts and examine secret motives. I give all people their due rewards according to what their actions deserve" (Jeremiah 17:9-10 NLT). We need to be concerned with the condition and orientation of our child's heart. If we focus only on how the externals are shaping our kids, we may miss out.

If we focus on protecting our kids, we tend to look at the negative elements. We tend to focus on the enemy. We seek ways to build barriers between our child and the perceived enemy. We develop a fortress mentality. "I don't want those bad people to break in and corrupt my kid." This is an *outside-in* mentality. It is externally oriented and concentrates on power. "I need to be more powerful and stronger than the enemy. I need to build an impenetrable fortress." This kind of thinking is usually driven by fear.

In contrast to the protection mindset, we opted for the preparation approach. This strategy also acknowledges enemy forces but sees them from without *and* within. An *inside-out* approach seeks to build strength within the heart of the child. The concentration is on the internals, not the externals.

A fortress mentality is static. "Stay in the bunker. Hide from the enemy. Don't venture out."

An *in-game* strategy is dynamic and portable. It can change and flex and go anywhere because it is inside of the child. It's not a place to hide but strength from within the heart of the child. It is based on authority, not power—the authority of who we are in Christ and the presence of the Holy Spirit indwelling us. We can send our kids off into the world with this authority, grounded on the Word of God. This gives us confidence. The in-game strategy is driven by faith, not fear. *Since our children are believers,* we were able to remind ourselves, *the same Holy Spirit that is in us is in them.*

DON'T MAKE IT TOO EASY ON THEM

Show me a woman who has discernment, and I'll show you a woman who has struggled. Show me a man who makes wise decisions, and I'll show you a man who made some bad decisions before he got to the wise ones.

For parents, it is tempting to make it easy on our kids. To insulate them against the harsh realities of the world. To isolate them from struggles. To shelter them. *Just because we had to toil doesn't mean our kids should have to.* It is easier to shelter kids and to raise them in an airtight environment than to try to raise them in the middle of the real world.

Sending our girls into the real world drove me to pray for them. It forced me to read the Bible. It compelled me to evaluate my parenting in light of biblical principles. It demanded that I stay engaged and connected with their lives. It required that I turn my heart toward theirs. It forced me to grow in my faith.

I discovered that God doesn't always remove the challenges. In fact, he usually uses the challenges to develop maturity, create dependency or test loyalty.

Consider the people of Israel as they were finally getting into the Promised Land after waiting forty years, or until the unfaithful generation died. Their parents had faced challenges, but this generation was known

> *It is our job as parents to train our children in warfare.*

for waiting. They had never faced battle. Their parents and grandparents had fought the battles. They were to inherit the land. How easy could it get? No work. No pain. No bloodshed.

But wait—why are these bad guys still around? "The LORD left certain nations in the land to test those Israelites who had not participated in the wars of Canaan. He did this to teach warfare to generations of Israelites who had no experience in battle" (Judges 3:1-2 NLT).

It is our job as parents to train our children in warfare. It may not be physical warfare, but it is at least spiritual, emotional and cultural warfare. There are certain enemies left in the land who will test your child. They aren't actors posing as enemies; they are real enemies.

There isn't safety with a fortress mentality. Real safety comes from being strong even amidst the enemy. Are you protecting your child, hoping that the enemy won't penetrate? Or are you preparing your child with discernment and skills for battle? You are either raising a wimp or preparing a warrior. Wimps or warriors, what will it be?

"I'm worried about my son Jared. He doesn't seem to have the motivation, discipline and perseverance that he'll need to make it in the world. He graduates in a few months, and I don't think he is ready," said Craig, a successful businessman.

"What have you done to prepare him to make wise decisions?"

"We gave him a cell phone and he ran up a huge bill. We gave him a car and he crashed it. He's not responsible."

"Any consequences to those?"

"Yeah, we took them away for a while."

"Does Jared have chores around the house?" I asked.

"Nah." Craig looked down at a tiny wrinkle on his starched dress shirt. "I know he should do something, but we don't make him. It's easier not to."

"I can see why you are worried. You should be. Jared isn't ready to be on his own. You've made it too easy on him. He's not disciplined as a warrior. Actually, he's a wimp."

"I know. He whines about everything."

"You need to change your approach. Tell him that it's going to be different in the next few months. Say that you are sorry for making it too easy on him. You realize that it has made him wimpy, and you want him to become a warrior. He may be offended, but it's true."

"Okay." Craig nodded. I could tell he was thinking.

"Craig, the struggles, the battles and the perseverance that you had in your twenties made you successful today. Don't rob Jared of the trials; they are good for him. By making it too easy on him, you are actually enabling him and making him weak. Set up situations where he has to make decisions and feel the results, the consequences of his choices. Through trial and error he will learn discernment. He will learn how to battle."

WELCOME TO BOOT CAMP

George Barna reports that four out of five U.S. parents (85 percent) believe they have the primary responsibility for the moral and spiritual development of their children, but more than two out of three of them abdicate that responsibility to their church.
Their virtual spiritual abandonment of their children is evident in how infrequently they engage in faith-oriented activities with their children. Fewer than 10 percent of parents who regularly attend church with their kids read the Bible together, pray together (other than at mealtimes) or participate in an act of service as a family unit. Most families do not have a genuine spiritual life together.[4]

Most families do not have a genuine spiritual life together.

Wimps or warriors? How can we prepare warriors if we have delegated the responsibility to someone else, and then only on a part-time basis?

Dear parent, I have two things to say: (1) It's your job to train your child morally and spiritually. The church should support you in that, but it's mostly your job. (2) It's not too late to start.

Craig went home from his consultation with me and had a discussion with Jared. He admitted that he had been off the mark in his role as a dad. He had thought that it was his job to protect and provide for his son, but he now realized at this stage he needed to be more about preparing and less about providing. In fact, Craig told him that he was going to change his orientation from making life *comfortable* to making Jared *ready*.

At first, Jared was shocked; life had been easy for him, and he was used to all of the creature comforts. But at some level he knew he needed to prepare for the next stage of life, even if that meant giving up some of his cushy life.

Craig met with another dad to discuss how they could work together to prepare their graduating sons for college. They came up with a rough plan and sat down individually with their sons. Craig told Jared, "Between now and the time you leave for college, we want to give you more and more freedom each month, but we want to see you make wise choices as we let out the leash. Over the next four months we want to see you develop discernment—which is using your insight and judgment to make wise choices. Here are a few areas we'd like to discuss with you. . . . What do you think?"

By then Jared's mouth was open with amazement, but he jumped at the opportunity to "prove he was a man." He made some mistakes, but he made them with the safety net of being at home. He was able to debrief with his dad and learn from each of the mistakes. He gained discernment from these experiences. He learned to think more deeply and consequentially. He saw that his choices had consequences.

Jared sensed the urgency and his dad's commitment to prepare him for college. Deep down inside he knew that he must train to be a warrior. So he did.

9

Courageously Setting Boundaries

Eileen was one of the star student leaders in our church youth group. Blonde, pretty and bright, at seventeen she was an accomplished pianist with scholarship offers from premier universities. One day she sat down on the couch in my office and crossed her legs. She wore a powder-blue warm-up suit, even though it was a hot summer day.

"Thanks for coming to see me," I said. I noticed that her usually sparkly blue eyes were dull and gray.

"Sure, I always enjoy talking with you. You have always been there for me, especially when my parents divorced. What's up?" She looked smaller and frailer than I remembered—and I had seen her less than a week ago. She seemed to be shrinking daily.

"Eileen, I know you are deciding on a college now. I am proud of you, your excellent grades, how you've been a leader in our group, how you've grown spiritually, and how you use your musical talent in the group. I really am proud of you." I paused to let the words sink in.

She turn pink and looked down at her Nikes. "Thanks."

"I care about you, and what I have to say today is because I care. Eileen, sometimes I think you work too hard. Do you ever catch yourself wanting to make *everything* work out?"

"Yeah, I do. I thought, *If I'm good enough, my parents won't get a divorce. If I get all A's, they'll be proud of me.* I thought they would be so happy with me that they'd forget about their fighting." She picked at a fingernail.

"Exactly. That's why I wanted to talk with you. Your parents' divorce doesn't have anything to do with you. You didn't cause it. You could not rescue their marriage. It was their responsibility, not yours. You could never perform well enough to change it."

"I struggle with that. I think, *If only I had been better. If only I hadn't been so demanding. If only they didn't have to pay for all my lessons and my braces. If only I had a job and could help out with the finances.* I spend most of my day thinking of if-onlys." She dabbed at a tear.

"Does it help?"

"No, but it's a habit now."

"You like to control things, don't you?" I handed her a tissue.

"Yeah, but my home life is so out of control. I have to focus on all the other stuff."

"In your quest to be the perfect daughter, the perfect student, the perfect leader and the perfect musician, you discovered that you couldn't control everything, so you obsessed with what you could control. It filled your mind."

She blinked and snapped her head back in surprise. "Exactly! It's like you are reading my mind!"

"You can't control the craziness in your family, so you focused on your body and food, thinking that you could find relief. You wanted everything to be perfect, but it wasn't."

She stared at the carpet, shaking her head slowly.

"It's okay, Eileen. I care. I'm not judging you. I accept you. But I'm worried about you."

Slowly she raised her head. She looked pale and gaunt, as if she had just received terrible news from her medical doctor. "I just wanted to look good." The spell was broken. The secret was out. Light was penetrating the darkness of her eating disorder for the very first time.

"You wanted others to accept you, I know." I reached for her hand. "And we do—just the way you are. You don't have to be thin to be accepted. You don't even have to be a good student, or a good Christian, or a good pianist. You just have to be you. I like you."

She started to cry.

We talked about her obsession with being perfect to feel accepted. I helped her see that her drivenness was coming from a place of hurt. She didn't always have to be perfect, I told her. She could be angry, sad, worried or afraid. She didn't have to stuff those negative emotions and pretend they weren't there. I helped her see that she was assuming too much responsibility and that she needed some protection and a break. With God's support, I helped her see that she needed boundaries.

It took a while, but she came around to see that a boundaryless life had almost killed her. When she checked into a hospital for eating disorders, she was down to eighty-one pounds!

ORDER

God is a God of order. Each day is limited to twenty-four hours. The oceans have their borders. The earth has a defined orbit. The sun comes up in the east and sets in the west. Order is good. We need order.

But sometimes our world gets out of order—like Eileen's. Her life was out of control. She couldn't control what was happening in her family. She felt that she had to do something, so she worked at her grades, at being good and at being thin. She found it hard to say no. She assumed too much responsibility. After a while her life became a blur. She had lost any sense of order in her life.

Our kids need boundaries. Boundaries are necessary for a balanced and healthy life. A boundary is a line

Boundaries help identify us.

that marks what each person is responsible for and not responsible for. Boundaries help identify us.

Henry Cloud and John Townsend are the boundaries experts. They have written a bestselling book, *Boundaries: When to Say Yes, When to Say No, To Take Control of Your Life.*

> Boundaries define us. They define *what is me* and *what is not me.* A boundary shows me where I end and someone else begins, leading me to a sense of ownership. Knowing what I am to own and take responsibility for gives me freedom. If I know where my yard begins and ends, I am free to do with it what I like. Taking responsibility for my life opens up many different options. However, if I do not "own" my life, my choices and options become very limited.[1]

Boundaries are essential for protecting our lives and allowing us to discover personal freedom. We need boundaries to guard our emotions and our sense of self. Boundaries protect the heart.

> Keep vigilant watch over your heart;
>   *that's* where life starts. (Proverbs 4:23 *The Message*)

Boundaries also delineate what is not ours. For example, we have a small block wall between our front yard and our neighbor's. My lawn is on my side and his is on his side. I mow my yard and he mows his. Not once have I gone outside and found my neighbor doing lawn work in *my* yard. I'd be okay with it, but it's never happened! Why? Because we have a clearly defined property line—a boundary that helps him know his property and what he is responsible for versus what I am responsible for. The clear demarcation eliminates problems. What would happen if we weren't sure where the line went? What would happen if he moved it, extending his yard four feet onto my property?

When boundaries are clear and respected, we have fewer problems. But in Eileen's case, she wasn't clear on what was her property (responsibility) and what wasn't. In time she discovered that she was not responsible for other people's actions. She was responsible only for herself. She wasn't responsible for her mom and dad's marriage. Her therapists at the clinic helped her discover that we are responsible *to* others and *for* ourselves. But we are not responsible *for* others.

> *We are responsible to others and for ourselves. But we are not responsible for others.*

A LIBERATING INSIGHT

"I just recently discovered that my childhood has impacted my adult life," said Carolina, a fortysomething client in my coaching office. "Growing up as a kid, I was always trying to keep the peace between my mother and my dad. I'd say to her, 'Dad didn't mean it. He's just had too much to drink.' I tried to smooth things out. I assumed 110 percent responsibility for how things went and how people were feeling in my family."

"How has that affected you now?"

"Well, I did the same thing with my husband. I assumed all the responsibility, and it wasn't too long until I also assumed all of the blame. It was always my fault. It didn't matter if I wasn't in the room, if a dish broke it was *my* fault."

"So what did you do?"

"I'm learning that I need to be accountable to others; that's why I'm seeing you. I want to be responsible *to* others. I want to share and express, instead of stuff and steam. But I'm also responsible *for* myself. I need to take the initiative and stop playing the victim. But I don't have to be responsible *for* others. I have enough to do taking care of myself."

"It's easy to lose our balance between assuming too much responsibility and not enough," I affirmed.

"You know that. It's taken me six months," confessed Carolina. "But I now know the difference between what is mine and what isn't. For the first time in my life I feel free!" She smiled. "I don't feel guilty. You are right. It's a weight off my shoulders."

A LESSON FROM BACKPACKING

I used to backpack, about fifteen years and fifteen pounds ago. I remember how much help it was when someone came alongside me and lifted some of the weight off my shoulders. It was usually when we were going up steep switchbacks and the backpack felt as if it was filled with huge rocks. My buddy would extend his hand and lift the bottom of my backpack, bringing instant relief to my aching shoulders. He didn't assume all fifty pounds; he probably only exerted five or ten pounds of lift—but it was a huge encouragement to me, physically and emotionally.

That's what Galatians 6:2 is talking about: "Share each other's troubles and problems, and in this way obey the law of Christ" (NLT).

Come alongside someone and help lift his heavy burden. It's still his burden. You didn't take it off his back and place it on yours. You simply lightened the burden for a little bit.

Another verse helps us understand the balance of boundaries. Galatians 6:5 says, "Each of you must take responsibility for doing the creative best you can with your own life" *(The Message)*. Another translation is "Each one should carry his or her own load." *Load* here is an image meaning "daily responsibilities or behavior." Each person is responsible for his or her own conduct. Unlike the heavy "burdens" (the fifty-pound backpacks), the "load" is more like a daypack—you know, the kind you might use to carry your gear to the gym. We are expected to each carry our own daypack, but we can get help if our big backpack becomes burdensome.

In other words, don't be lazy and irresponsible and toss someone your daypack and say, "Hey, carry this for me, will you?" Keep your own load—your daypack—but be willing to lift the burden of someone who is struggling with a heavy weight. We are expected to "carry" our own emotions, attitudes and behaviors, even though it requires effort. We are also expected to pitch in at times and lift the burden of those feeling overwhelmed.

Problems arise when people pretend that heavy burdens (like divorce, loss of job, cancer, financial problems) are simply their daily load or daypack. They are trying to carry too heavy of a burden alone.

Others don't carry enough. These are the people who stay in a perpetual state of need because they imagine that their daypack is a crushing burden.

Don't confuse your burdens with your responsibilities and your responsibilities with your burdens.

BOUNDARIES WITH KIDS

We need to teach our kids boundaries so they don't struggle for forty years as Carolina did. In healthy families every family member knows where he begins and ends. He knows what he is responsible for and what he is not. There is order. The expectations are clear and realistic. They don't change with the weather. They aren't so idealistic that they drive kids to be fake and externally focused. Parents' expectations have as much to do with the child's inner life, or heart, as they do the child's behavior, performance and external life.

I'm a family systems person. I look for systems in my family and in other families that make it work or not work. We all have these systems; they are usually developed from expectations, roles, responsibilities, values and boundaries. In some families the systems are healthy and address the needs of every family member. In other words, the family works. In other families the system is actually toxic because it is hurtful to some or all of the family members.

This isn't some new pop-psychology spiel. It's as old as the Pentateuch. In fact, it's part of the Ten Commandments:

> Don't bow down to them and don't serve them because I am GOD, your God, and I'm a most jealous God, punishing the children for any sins their parents pass on to them to the third, and yes, even to the fourth generation of those who hate me. But I'm unswervingly loyal to the thousands who love me and keep my commandments. (Exodus 20:5-6 *The Message*)

Who wants to be stuck with their parents' sin? It's like having to pay their bill when you walk into a restaurant, before you eat, because they had run up a tab. It's not fair, especially to our Western way of thinking, which highlights the free agency of individuals and plays down family responsibilities and duty.

It may not seem fair, but it's true. Our parents' foibles, prejudices, idiosyncrasies and sin are passed on to us. We don't have to pick them up and make them our own, but in all likelihood, unless we think about it and make careful choices, we will pattern ourselves after our parents.

There is terrific good news in the second part of the Scripture. God's love is for a thousand generations! The curse and craziness of your family may affect it for three for four generations, but God's love will influence it for *a thousand generations!* The good news is that *the blessing is greater than the curse.*

Say it aloud: The blessing is greater than the curse.

Liberating, isn't it? You may come from a wacko family, but you don't have to pass that same craziness, addiction and boundaryless existence on to your kids. It's your choice. You can be the transitional generation.

> Today I am giving you the choice between a blessing and a curse! You will be blessed if you obey the commands of the LORD your God that I am giving you today. You will receive a curse if you reject the commands of the LORD your God and turn from his way by worshiping foreign gods. (Deuteronomy 11:26-28 NLT)

When we raise our kids with a commitment to develop Godlike character qualities within them, and when we model these qualities before them, we empower them to withstand the foreign gods that are within our land. We bless them with strength. We bless them with wisdom. We bless them with a rich spiritual legacy that will enhance their lives long after we are gone.

Looking forward involves looking back. Cloud and Townsend remind us:

> The patterns you learn at home growing up are continued into

adulthood with the same players: lack of consequences for irre-sponsible behavior, lack of confrontation, lack of limits, taking responsibility for others instead of yourself, giving out of com-pulsion and resentment, envy, passivity, and secrecy. These pat-terns are not new; they have just never been confronted and repented of.

These patterns run deep. Your family members are the ones you learned to organize your life around, so they are able to send you back to old patterns by their very presence. You begin to act automatically out of *memory* instead of growth.

To change, you must identify these "sins of the family" and turn from them. You must confess them as sins, repent of them, and change the way you handle them. The first step in estab-lishing boundaries is becoming aware of old family patterns that you are still continuing in the present.[2]

Courage

Boundaries are courage in action. Boundaries are courage in rela-tionships.

From the beginning I have wanted my daughters to be coura-geous. I know that the old medieval myth was for the princess to be in the tower, weeping helplessly, and finally to be rescued by a male knight in shining armor, but I didn't like that imagery. Why couldn't the princess throw a few punches and get *herself* out of the tower? Why couldn't she use her beauty and brains to find her way out? And why was she stuck in the tower in the first place? I didn't buy it. If anything, I wanted our daughters to be on the horse rescuing others. I mean, why settle for victim when you can be the victor? We are drawn to strong and courageous female characters.

I wanted our girls to be courageous. I knew that if they could be strong and know where to draw the line, they wouldn't be taken advantage of *even though they are girls.* Actually, I was more militant than that. My biggest fear was that people, particularly males, would take advantage of them—emotionally, sexually and mentally. I wanted to instill such confidence in them that it would scare away the flakes. When a girl is insecure, she attracts the losers and the manipulators.

I wanted to see our daughters be strong and courageous enough to repel those with evil intentions but attract those with noble character. *It takes one to know one.*

Boundaries are courage in action.

As our kids get ready to posses the land of their own lives, they need boundaries.

> Be strong and courageous, for you will lead my people to possess all the land I swore to give their ancestors. Be strong and very courageous. Obey all the laws Moses gave you. Do not turn away from them, and you will be successful in everything you do. Study this Book of the Law continually. Meditate on it day and night so you may be sure to obey all that is written in it. Only then will you succeed. I command you—be strong and courageous! Do not be afraid or discouraged. For the LORD your God is with you wherever you go. (Joshua 1:6-8 NLT)

Do you actually believe this text? Do you honestly believe that "God is with you wherever you go"? If you do, you will have the strength and courage to parent with boundaries. If your children are believers, you will be able to instill courage in them because God is with them. You may not be with them, but God is with them. As noted earlier, I like to remind myself, *The same Holy Spirit that is in me is in my child.*

A child who is courageously setting boundaries will

- be able to resist negative peer pressure
- have a clearly defined sense of self, knowing who she is and what is important to her
- be able to see beyond his immediate social setting
- be self-confident, courageous and capable
- less likely to be involved in at-risk behavior (sex, drugs and alcohol)
- process life's disappointments and not be overwhelmed by them
- not be intimidated by bosses, teachers, coaches or others who are unjust, mean or insecure
- likely have a positive view of authority, knowing that God ordains it for order

If you have teenagers, I think it's appropriate to have a discussion in which you ask each other, "Where in our life could we use a boundary? Where do I give in where I should say no?"

They might say, "Mom, you don't have to do the Snack Shack at every one of my games. You do too much. Let the other parents step up."

You might say, "You don't always have to be the one who does cleanup after youth group. I wind up waiting for you for thirty minutes each week. Tell the youth director you'll do it every other week."

Your teen might say, "Dad, you are on three committees at church, and I know you hate two of them. Why not quit those and just stay on the one you love?"

A parent might say, "How come you always have to pick up Ginger? Why can't she drive some of the time?"

See how it works?

Sometimes it's simply a matter of not seeing our blind spot. Teens love to point these out, by the way. So serve it back to them. Get a little volley going. Keep it light and offer it as a suggestion, and be willing to walk away from it. Remember, the goal is for the child, especially a teenager, to set boundaries for *herself,* not you.

A parent who is courageously setting boundaries might

- not work on the weekends, but instead spend time with the family
- set aside money each month for a fun summer vacation for the family
- budget grocery money and with the savings support a child in need
- limit the number of times the family eats out
- limit the number of enrichment and after-school activities for the kids
- turn down a job that would require a long commute
- set limits for video games, TV and the Internet
- exercise regularly and eat a healthy diet
- avoid gambling, tobacco, alcohol, soap operas and anything that might be addictive
- begin each day by praying and reading God's Word to gain the strength and wisdom needed for the day

THE CONCERT

When we really believe that God is with our child, we allow her to make her own choices. We empower our child when we train her to courageously set her own boundaries.

This is difficult, because sometimes our children make the wrong choice. We want to rush in and rescue them from the pain and hassle, but we shouldn't.

Brooke is a gifted student and athlete. When she was in high school, she was on a championship volleyball team. She played club volleyball and was on her school team. She was skilled as a middle blocker, and we loved watching her play. But she was also a loyal friend. She has nurtured a dozen friendships over the years, some dating back to kindergarten, and she is now in college. One of her long-term friends gave her an early birthday present: tickets to see Jack Johnson, a popular singer, in concert in Santa Barbara. They planned the special outing months in advance.

About halfway into the volleyball season, the schedule was changed, and a big game against our rivals was moved to the same night as the concert. Brooke came to Suzanne and me. "What should I do? Jen bought these tickets, and they are expensive. We've been planning this for months. I didn't know there was going to be a conflict!"

My first inclination was to say that she had a responsibility to the team and that she should tell Jen thanks but she would not be able to go. But as Suzanne and I discussed it, we reminded each other that we had raised Brooke to be grateful for gifts and loyal to friends and to actually enjoy her high school years—it doesn't always have to be about performance. The next day we told her, "We are leaving the decision up to you. Whatever you decide, we will support. You are a senior and have the maturity to make the right call. If you decide to go to the concert, you do need to let the coach know in time for him to make adjustments before the game."

I expected her to skip the concert and play in the game. Being the old jock that I am, that is what I would have done.

But she told Jen that she'd go with her to the concert. She told her coach that she would not be able to play in the big game because of a previous commitment and that the conflict had come up due to the rescheduling.

He was furious. He uttered a few words that weren't in the dictionary and challenged Brooke about her priorities.

But she courageously stuck with her boundary. She told him, "Friends and previous commitments are important—sorry."

You may not agree with her decision. I'm not sure I do. But that's the point: it was *her* decision, and we supported her in it. She went to the concert and had a fun time.

Her coach sulked and responded with immaturity. Without her the team lost to its rival, and that made him angrier. As payback he didn't start Brooke for the rest of the season. He glared at us whenever we saw him.

There are costs to boundaries. Brooke's decision cost her the honor of starting, but her courage and setting of boundaries gave her a lesson for life.

10

Choosing Contentment

Mix a little foolishness with your prudence;
it's good to be silly at the right moment.

HORACE

Perhaps I've made the epigraph above my life motto—and I think some people have pictures to prove it. That worries me. I've been known to be foolish and not always at the right moment. But that's okay. In the long run, I'd rather have my kids smile, say, "Yeah, that's my dad," and be slightly embarrassed, than to frown and painfully admit only to being a distant relative.

I figure it's payback time anyway. They embarrass us when they are little with things like picking their nose in the photo published in the church photo directory. So when they're teens, we embarrass them by simply being on the planet. It's fair.

You've probably heard the saying "Children are messages we deliver to a future we may never see." Okay, it's slightly depressing. But the fact is, as parents, we are preparing future adults who are preparing for future families. Why not send them into the future smiling? Let's make our homes dens of laughter. Let's model contentment to our kids. Let's show them how to be joyful.

This book is really about raising joyful children. If our kids develop the personal qualities of vision, authenticity, listening, empathy, compassion, discernment and boundaries, they are going to enjoy life. They will be able to spend their time embracing life and people, rather than looking for the next buzz and using people. They won't give in to the diversions of sex, drugs and rock 'n' roll. (Okay, they may give in to rap, country or hip-hop though.)

EMBRACING CONTENTMENT

To embrace contentment, you have to have the freedom to be different, a preference for humor and a default setting of gratefulness. If you have these three qualities, you will have a joyful home.

An unhappy home focuses on what we don't have. There tends to be a lot of whining—and parents can be whiny too, not just kids. The opposite of a whiny family is a contented one.

How do we learn and teach contentment?

Contentment isn't necessarily comfort. Don't make things too easy on your kids; if you do, you may be robbing them of genuine contentment:

A sense of competence and self-confidence comes from responsibility. Financial advisors counsel wealthy parents not to let their hired help make the kids' beds, clean their rooms, brush the dog or load the dishwasher; all chores the children can handle themselves. Instead, give the children chores and have regular family meetings to get everyone in the habit of talking things out, parents included. Whether those first discussions are about where to go on vacation or how to improve the neighborhood, the idea is to build relationships and skills before kids end up on the board of the family foundation with power to spend, spend, spend.[1]

Contentment has been defined as *discovering peace with who I am and what I have*. It's not just about material possessions. It's not about wealth. The root of genuine contentment is actually spiritual. I've met contented people in decaying, high-rise tenement walk-ups in Romania and in mud-and-stick huts in Honduras. Their contentment was based not on their situation but on their perspective. The contented families I've met overseas consistently focus on grace and what they are grateful for; they seldom have time to think about what they *don't* have. In some ways they are richer than people in North America. Tim Stafford pinpoints our poverty of discontent:

> Some people spend their entire life plagued by a state of discontent. Their spouse disappoints them. They don't like their job. They wish for different looks. Their children let them down. Their friends aren't in the circle they would like. I've known people, and you probably have too, who become so sour that nobody wants to be around them. They are "glass-half-empty" people. It has little to do with what they have or what they achieve. It has to do with a deeper, spiritual condition. If we could pass on the secret of contentment to our children, what gift could be more valuable?[2]

Contentment will help us and our children learn how to pace our lives and avoid overscheduling them. Contentment provides us with the means to a simpler lifestyle. Contentment helps us avoid the consumer debt pit. It helps us remember that the fact that we see something we'd like doesn't mean we have to buy it on credit.

Contentment is a spiritual state that promotes spiritual disciplines and is strengthened by them. Contentment is fueled by the disciplines of reading of Scripture, prayers of thanksgiving, fasting, giving to others, learning about others in need, praying for them and giving service to those in need. These are the pathways to contentment.

One family keeps a blank book at the kitchen table to record "blessings" each day. They begin each day by writing down at least one thing they are grateful for; then at dinner they write another. Each year they accumulate more than seven hundred reasons that they should be content. Contentment begins with the little things.

It's so easy to become focused on what we don't have. We are bombarded by marketing that is designed to appeal to and foster our dissatisfaction: if only you had our product, you'd be happier, sexier, have better hair, clearer skin or more friends. Scripture's call goes exactly counter to this: "Don't be obsessed with getting more material things. Be relaxed with what you have. Since God assured us, 'I'll never let you down, never walk off and leave you'" (Hebrews 13:5 *The Message*).

Contentment is being relaxed with what we have. It is knowing that what is most important can never be taken away. It is the assurance that we will be provided for and never abandoned. God will never leave us. With that we can be content.

DON'T TAKE YOURSELF TOO SERIOUSLY—YOUR KIDS DON'T

Most of this book is about serious stuff, but this may be the most important chapter for you. You may need to lighten up as a parent. You may need to discover your lost funny bone. You may need to put the book down for a while and turn on Comedy Central. After all, you may need a break. It's like the sage and actor Ed Asner said, "Raising kids is part joy and part guerrilla warfare."

Here again, it bears repeating: *play is a*

> *Raising kids is part joy and part guerrilla warfare.*
>
> **Ed Asner**

child's economy. Kids trade in fun. Adults trade in time and cash, as in "billable hours" or "hourly rates." But kids think in the capital of fun. A child's economic criterion is *will it be fun?*

I have found this to be universally true. In any socioeconomic setting, in North America or abroad, kids like to have fun. If this is the case, why aren't we harnessing fun's power for the good of our family? Why aren't we leveraging our children's penchant for fun? It seems to me that the more fun we can have with our children, the more influence we will have on them. And in some cases, we may have more influence with the fun stuff than with the serious stuff (even the serious stuff in this book).

> *The more fun we can have with our child, the more influence we will have on him or her.*

Girls just wanna have fun. Boys too. I learned this way before I heard the song on the radio. As a youth worker, I discovered that if you are friendly, know kids' names and have fun, you can teach them moral and spiritual truths. But you can't skip the fun and go straight to the heavy stuff. We devised goofy and at times foolish skits, stunts, games and videos to generate laughter. These seldom had a point; if there was a point, it was stretched like Gumby's legs to make it connect to the lesson of the day. But that didn't matter. When kids laugh, they open their hearts. When kids laugh, they open their minds. When kids laugh, they relax and feel a part of the group or the family. So let's laugh!

You may be thinking, *I'm an engineer; we are programmed to not be funny.* Or, *There is so much wrong with the world. We should be serious.*

Let me offer you a shocking insight that may help: Your kids are already laughing at you—you may as well join them! If your kids are eight or older, rest assured they have funny memories of you. You may not think so, but they do! Why not go with the flow and join the humor?

SEVEN WAYS HUMOR HELPS

1. Humor helps you not to take life or yourself too seriously.

2. Humor helps you feel connected as a family.

3. Humor helps reduce stress.

4. Humor is healing. "A cheerful heart is good medicine" (Proverbs 17:22).

5. Humor gives you perspective. *This too shall pass.*

6. Humor builds memories. "Do you remember the time . . . ?"

7. Humor makes you more human and more approachable.

Phil McGraw, TV personality and writer, joins me in the plea for more family humor: "If you want to raise children who have the ability to laugh at life's insanity, you've got to help them see life's funny side. How much fun are you to live with?"[3]

One of the qualities of a healthy family is the presence of laughter, usually with plenty of inside family stories to swap. "Remember the time Dad was lost and pulled into a driveway and pulled out his roadmap, only to discover that he had parked in front of a fire station? He only realized it when the siren went off and the doors rolled up and the firemen stood there stunned: *Some guy is parked in front of us?*" (True story.) "Or how about the time Bingo fell out of our SUV with his leash on and ran alongside the car at forty-five miles per hour so he wouldn't get run over?" (Another true story.) "Then there was the first time I introduced my bride-to-be to my grandma. I said, 'I want you to meet Suzanne, my fiancée, Grandma.' And she responded, 'Nice to meet you, Grandma.' I had to remind her, 'No, *you* are Grandma; this is Suzanne.'"

Keeping these humorous moments alive by retelling the stories reminds us that we are a nutty family, but we love and respect one another—and next time the story may be on you.

DIFFERENT DOESN'T HAVE TO BE WEIRD

Healthy families allow children to be different.

The freedom to be funny is also the freedom to be different. We don't have to march lockstep as the perfect, standardized Christian family. As I see it, there's room for all kinds of families. There isn't one cookie-cutter form for "the perfect Christian family." As Grandma used to say, "It takes all types."

Healthy families allow children to be different. It's a sign that the family is grace based as opposed to performance based. Tim Kimmel talks about differentness in *Grace-Based Parenting:*

> Let me give you some synonyms for "different" so that you clearly understand what I'm referring to. I'm talking about "unique," "weird,' "bizarre," "strange," "goofy," and "quirky." Grace-based homes should provide a safe haven for these kinds of children. . . . But those who are just plain different and do goofy things aren't necessarily wrong. They're just *different.* Because their different looks or behavior often annoy or embarrass their parents, it is automatically assumed that whatever they are doing (or want to do) must not be tolerated. This makes it tough for kids hard-wired by God to be a bit different and limits us in being used as God's instruments of grace. I defend the right of children to be different if for no other reason than the

fact that they are *children*. They are young. Their hearts stir with an almost miraculous sense of wonder. Their young minds run wild and sometimes perform crazy gauntlets within their imaginations. God made them this way.[4]

Sometimes our kids' being different is intentionally annoying. Their dress is intended to make us gasp. I'm thinking, for example, of the current rage of huge, baggy pants that can't seem to stay on boys' hips but sag low and make you think that they have all become plumbers.

Sure, the fashion is outlandish, and some of the music sounds like two freight trains having a head-on collision. And the hairstyles and colors look like something a preschooler would get in trouble for. Still, allow your young 'uns the freedom to be different with the things that don't last, even if their style irritates you. Here's a principle I've found that helps me to choose my battles carefully and maintain a sense of humor: Let them express themselves. Just take plenty of pictures!

MANSION MANIA

I have a client that builds big houses—I'm talking thirty-five-thousand-square-foot homes on up. In the Los Angeles market! They cost twenty-five to fifty million dollars, and values are rising. One day he brought his portfolio of photos to show me the intricate woodwork, exquisite stone and marble, the state-of-the-art technology, the spectacular pools. And that's just on the first floor!

It was impressive.

As I gasped in awe, he ruminated: "Not one of these families is happy. They have all the money in the world and a new, high-end home, and they are not content. They are some of the most critical, whiny people I've met—and every one of them has a lousy marriage. I know, 'cause I often get caught in the middle of it."

I couldn't believe it at first. How could you *not* be happy living in paradise? How could you not be content with all that opulence? I think I'd be happy living just in the game room of one of these mansions! Then it occurred to me: Contentment is a mindset, not a standard of living. These folks raised their standard of living but had not raised their contentment level. They were bound to be disappointed.

How sad it would be to design your dream home, expecting that it would bring you happiness, only to discover that it didn't. *The driveway doesn't angle quite right. The chandelier in the entry is too small. The marble in the powder room is too pink. The spa doesn't have enough jets.*

> *Contentment is a mindset, not a standard of living.*

Yeah, I could see how it would be a letdown.

CONTENTMENT IS NOT MEDIOCRITY

Driven people often confuse contentment with mediocrity. "What do you mean, be content with what I have? That's laziness. You should always want more."

Contentment and laziness are on a continuum. One can look like the other. I'm not advocating, of course, that we teach our kids to be lazy. (They seem to come by that naturally, anyway.) I want my kids to be ambitious, but for the right reasons. Hugh Hewitt says it well in his excellent book *In but Not Of: A Guide to Christian Ambition and the Desire to Influence the World:* "The reality for all Christians is the obligation to equip themselves for their greatest impact and to seek every opportunity to increase that impact. And never to suspect that they are not called or that their time has passed them by."[5]

I don't want my kids to be okay with a mediocre life. I want them to be influencers. I want them to be change agents. I want them to be courageous kingdom builders for God. I want them to be content, but not with mediocrity. Paul urges us to be ambitious *for noble purposes:* "I know how to live on almost nothing or with everything. I have learned the secret of living in every situation, whether it is with a full stomach or empty, with plenty or little. For I can do everything with the help of Christ who gives me the strength I need" (Philippians 4:12-13 NLT).

I want my kids to be content, but not with mediocrity.

Contentment is rooted in faith. It's not dependent on circumstances; it's dependent on my perspective—am I trusting in my comfort or in Christ for my contentment?

I want my kids to know the secret of living in every situation. Don't you? That quality is valuable and transferable. Contentment helps us relax and perform well because we aren't stressed about the details of our life, as Stafford explains:

> If you trust, failure doesn't disable you; you know the results don't depend just on you. I want my children to grow up ambitious because they trust God to do wonderful things.
>
> If I were to draw a portrait of contentment, it wouldn't show somebody lying in a hammock, sipping lemonade. I would show a baseball player at bat, confident in his abilities, sure that he is meant to be in this joyful spot. He won't get a hit every time, but he knows that he will get his share. He wants to succeed, but not in order to show himself as better than the rest of his team. He wants to contribute to his team. Therefore he is happy and relaxed as he focuses on the ball and swings with all his skill and strength.[6]

Contentment is a choice. It's not something that *happens to* someone; it's something that a person chooses. He decides to be content. He is focusing on what he can control—swinging the bat. Not what he can't control—the fan booing in the second level. Each of us, even the mansion owners, has something that can make us discontent. Each of us has something that can make us content: another day to enjoy and to own.

Contentment is a choice.

We own our own life. No one else has a deed to our life. We can embrace what is given us and make the most of it. We shouldn't take anything for granted. Each day is a gift. With that alone we should be content.

Each day affords us a basic menu. We make a choice to be content or discontent.

A contented parent

- chooses to be grateful for his job, even though it is stressful—it is less stressful than being unemployed

- chooses to accept his children as-is and doesn't make his acceptance conditional

- wants the best for her child, doesn't accept mediocrity, but is content to allow time for process and growth over time

- understands that some kids are average students but that doesn't make them less exceptional human beings

- realizes that true contentment has more to do with satisfaction of the soul than possession of goods

- will sometimes say "That's enough" and mean it, putting a stop to the cycle of acquiring

- knows that real joy and contentment come from relationships, not things, and makes people a priority

- works at maintaining friendships and takes time to enjoy them

If we choose contentment and model it in front of our kids, we can expect to see children who choose contentment—children who

- aren't caught up in having to own the latest toy, gadget or fashion
- are satisfied with simple things
- feel free to laugh and be themselves, and be silly if they want to
- have a strong sense of initiative and ambition tempered with the ability to pace themselves and relax
- aren't trying to prove their worth with their grades or athletic or musical performance but have a deep sense of personal worth and competence
- understand and embrace serenity rather than an anxious pursuit of "what's hot"
- are grateful for their home and their school, even though they are not as desirable as the ones on the teen TV shows
- accept their parents as they are, knowing they aren't perfect but accepting them unconditionally
- are thankful and appreciative of their friends, knowing that the key to being content lies in connecting rather than consuming

11

Loving Passionately

It's easy to talk with you. It's weird," Stephanie mused. "I feel comfortable here." She spread out on the loveseat in my family-coaching office, dangling her long legs over the side.

"That's the point. Make yourself at home."

"Now why would I want to do that? Home is the most *un*comfortable place. My parents are wacked. They don't have a clue. They're stress cases."

"They brought you here," I offered.

"Yeah, you're right—but honestly, I can never find someone to talk with. You're the first. Nobody knows how I'm feeling. Or maybe they know, but they don't care? Heck, I dunno. But I do know it feels good to be here, to talk with you . . . but it's weird."

"I know. It is weird. Not something you do every day."

She smiled. At seventeen she had an attractive smile—her parents had paid thousands of dollars for it. Her braces had come off just a few months earlier. She fiddled with her red hair, checking for split ends. "You know, my parents *think* they get me, but they don't. They're clueless. They don't know what I'm going through. They say they do, but they really don't. So I usually keep it all inside, but then I freak out. I lose it. I take it out on people around me."

"I know. That's what got you in here in the first place. But you are talking about it now. That's cool. That's what you need. You don't want to be alone with all of this stuff. You don't want to have to make sense of it by yourself."

"Exactly!" She bobbed her head, sending her long auburn locks forward and back. "I can chill now that I have someone to talk to. I'm already a fiery redhead. I don't need to be some volcano vixen."

I laughed, "Yeah, let's work on that."

Stephanie is just one of the many teens and children that I have talked with in the last few years who feel unloved and disconnected. She lives in a nice home, attends a nice school, has nice parents—but does not feel nice. Her parents had grounded her for coming in late, whereupon she starting throwing kitchen appliances and knives at her mom at one-thirty in the morning. That was why they had brought her to see me. "When I saw the toaster barely miss my mom's head and splat into a million pieces when it hit the wall, I realized just how ticked off I was," she admitted.

We may be raising the most disconnected generation.

Her parents kept busy with their own lives and assumed that keeping their daughter busy would keep her out of trouble. But their hectic schedules only reinforced her loneliness and lack of connection. They were clueless regarding how to understand and help their teenage daughter. They found it easier to give her cash than to risk spending time with her.

Stephanie represents the overindulged, unloved kids of our culture. We may be raising the most disconnected generation of modern times. As a Gallup research fellow, I have worked with George Gallup to design and interpret surveys of America's youth. On our research for my book *The Seven Cries of Today's Teens*,[1] we discovered that 93 percent of the youth surveyed said that "the need to be understood and loved" was an "important" or "very important" need in their life. This was second to "to be trusted," by only half a percent. The distinction is practically irrelevant. On any given day it is safe to assume that our kids want to be trusted *and* loved.

> *Our kids are growing up in a culture that is extremely antichildren.*

But many are not feeling loved. In his book *Hurt: Inside the World of Today's Teenagers*, youth worker and professor Chap Clark writes, "Adolescents need adults to become adults, and when adults are not present and involved in their lives, they are forced to figure out how to survive life on their own."[2]

Our kids want to connect with us. As noted earlier, over 70 percent would love to spend more time with their father, and 85 percent of teens would like to have a mentor.[3] Our kids are growing up in a culture that is extremely antichildren. They are afraid of being abandoned by their parents. They need guides through the fears of childhood and the maze of adolescence.

SELF-CARE FOR CONNECTING

To nurture and guide your child, you will first need to nurture yourself as the parent. If parents are to provide a supportive, positive and loving environment in which their children can accomplish their developmental tasks, they will have to grow in the areas of their own emotional weaknesses. Perhaps you did not grow up in a loving, nurturing family. You may struggle with loving your child. You may struggle with hurt, resentment and anger from your past. If this is your situation, the first step is to deal with your own hurt and lack of love. You can't give to your child what you don't have.

Dealing with your past might involve reading books, checking out websites, joining groups, attending seminars, or getting personal counseling or coaching. It is never too late to receive healing from the wounds of your past. It is a hassle and will require an investment, and it will sting a little. But you should do it for the sake of your children. Your kids deserve your best, and your best is not likely if you have not dealt with the pain of your past.

Loving our kids isn't always easy. Sometimes I find myself "on empty" when it comes to *feeling* love for my kids or for my wife. At such times I don't feel very loving. I don't feel very caring. I just want to be alone and take care of myself. To reach out to someone else requires energy, and some days I simply don't feel energetic. When I recognize this, I try to take an assessment of my heart: *Why am I on empty? What has been draining my emotional tank? What can I do to refuel my soul? Do I need to be alone? Do I need exercise? Do I need to rest?*

Most of the time, I realize that I'm stretched too thin and thus don't have the emotional reserves to really love my family. I need to fill up the reservoir. A trip to the gym or going surfing usually restores me emotionally. Sometimes a few minutes reflecting on God's Word or musing over a well-written book will refuel me.

As parents, we need to know what are our energy drainers (probably the kids!) and what are our energy restorers. We need to make time to restore our own soul if we are going to have the emotional reserves for our kids. It's not selfish to take care of ourselves emotionally and physically; it's strategic.

KIDS NEED TO CONNECT

Love is the foundation for a healthy life. Kids discover how to love, or not love, at home. The love relationship between the parent and the child is critical. We determine our

Our kids need to be loved by someone who chooses to love them.

child's sense of worth, the climate of our home and the future success of our child by whether or not we have a loving relationship with him or her. In the words of David Popenoe, professor of sociology at Rutgers University and cochair of the Council on Families in America, "Children develop best when they are provided the opportunity to have warm, intimate, continuous, and enduring relationships with both their fathers and their mothers."[4]

Our kids need to be loved by someone who chooses to love them. They need to be loved by someone who sees in them something worth loving. They need to see unconditional love modeled in the home. Unconditional love means, "I will always love you, no matter what." It doesn't depend on your behavior, your grades, how well you perform, if you are a gifted athlete or even if you have a good attitude. *I will always love you.*

Every week kids say to me, "It's never enough for my parent. I do better in one area, and they bring up something bad about something else. So why bother? Why try?"

Unconditional love means accepting the child and correcting the behavior. It doesn't mean winking at bad behavior. It means loving our kids enough to see them grow. As our kids enter their teen years, they will be in hot pursuit of individuation—which means becoming their own individual apart from you, their parent. This isn't rebellion, though it may look like it. This isn't rejection, though it may feel like it. It is a necessary and challenging developmental task for teens. *Who am I?* becomes a preoccupation in their minds. *Am I weird or normal, cool or uncool?* also plagues their brains.

Here's how to respond. Say, "Even if you are weird, I still love you." And if they are doing outlandish things with their hair, fashion or body to look "different" (which always happens to be like most of their friends), say, "I love you, regardless of your hair, clothes or friends." Then, the real test of unconditional love comes when you can say (and really mean it), "I love you unconditionally, even if you break the rules and don't follow my advice. I will love you even if you are a rebel."

In *Why Christian Kids Rebel,* Kimmel explores one of the many reasons our teens need our unconditional love *and* our modeling of love for others:

> Here's the problem: disdain for the things of the world can slip across a thin line and become disdain for the *people* in the world. Children that grow up in homes where parents are quick to speak critically about people caught up in the world's way of thinking are going to have a tough time personally appropriating God's grace. If grace is not shown toward the people who need it most, how are kids going to learn to show it in their day-to-day involvement with others, including their own parents?[5]

Unconditional love means loving our kids when they deserve it the least. It actually is a theological principle. Unconditional love is grace in action. I define grace as "love in relationship." God loved us so much that he didn't want anything to interfere with the relationship, so in grace he provided Christ as the payment/bridge between humans and himself. We didn't earn salvation; it was a gift of grace.

Christ arrives right on time to make this happen. He didn't, and doesn't, wait for us to get ready. He presented himself for this sacrificial death when we were far too weak and rebellious to do anything to get ourselves ready. . . . But God put his love on the line for us by offering his Son in sacrificial death while we were of no use whatever to him. (Romans 5:6-8 *The Message*)

Unconditional love is really grace in action.

Not only do our kids learn about love at home, they also learn about grace. Their very first perceptions of God will be shaped by their view of their mother and father. Is he loving? Is she forgiving? Is he angry? Is she critical?

How we model love for our kids will influence if they will be able to love us back and have an intimate, trusting faith with their heavenly Father.

WHAT IS LOVING PASSIONATELY?

Love is both tough and tender. Love is generously giving grace for the moment and wisdom for the future. Love provides the climate for kids to grow. A lack of love stunts normal healthy development.

I was thinking about the relationship between love, growth and unity. It occurred to me that the healthiest homes aren't the ones without the problems; the healthiest families I know are the ones that love each other in the midst of their troubles. They are the ones that create an atmosphere for growth with unconditional love. And as a result, they enjoy unity.

The healthiest homes aren't the ones without the problems; the healthiest families I know are the ones that love each other in the midst of their troubles.

Scripture details the elements of a healthy home and a loving parent:

- *Patience.* "Be humble and gentle. Be patient with each other, making allowance for each other's faults because of your love" (Ephesians 4:2 NLT). A loving parent will be patient with his child, knowing that it takes time to grow, learn and acquire skills and abilities.

- *Atmosphere for Growth.* ". . . Until we come to such unity in our faith and knowledge of God's Son that we will be mature and full grown in the Lord, measuring up to the full stature of Christ" (Ephesians 4:13 NLT). An atmosphere of growth keeps in mind that the standard is Christ and we are seeking to grow to become more like him. "Until we come" implies that we are all in process. Our homes are to be "greenhouses" for growth and development.

- *Security and stability.* "Then we will no longer be like children, forever changing our minds about what we believe because someone has told us something different or because someone has cleverly lied to us and made the lie sound like the truth" (Ephesians 4:14 NLT).

Stability and consistency are marks of maturity. We hope to see them more and more in our children. We are more likely to see them if we are consistent ourselves. One of the most frustrating behaviors for a child is for her parent to be always changing his mind. Modeling consistency, even when the child is presenting many challenges, is a practical way of demonstrating love. In effect you are saying, "I love you too much to give into your demands."

If the atmosphere of a home is volatile and charged with tension, people will not be getting along. Stability provides a predictable environment where unity can thrive.

The key to growing loving kids is to help them know and mature in Christ. Love then becomes a manifestation of their relationship with God.

> See how very much our heavenly Father loves us, for he allows us to be called his children, and we really are! But the people who belong to this world don't know God, so they don't understand that we are his children. Yes, dear friends, we are already God's children. (1 John 3:1 NLT)

My definition of love: *Love takes the initiative and acts sacrificially to meet the needs of the other person.*

Love makes the first move. It doesn't wait to respond; it acts.

Love is willing to make a sacrifice. It isn't about trading, or keeping things even.

Love studies the other person enough to know her needs and is willing to meet them.

Love provides the atmosphere for people to grow. When people are growing, they get along, they feel connected. We want to foster a climate of love in our home. When people feel loved, they are willing to grow, but when they feel unloved, they become defensive and closed to growth and change.

When each family member makes a commitment to love the others by meeting the needs of the others, unity prevails. It's not a formula but a process, and the process looks like this:

Love —> Growth —> Unity.

Love provides the atmosphere for growth, which leads to unity in the family. Love grows a relationship between parent and child that can last a lifetime.

It's about being there. I like the way my friend John Trent describes it:

Being there is about going beyond casual acquaintances to make deep, lasting connections. To be there for someone adds a sense of mission and purpose to our lives, even as it subtracts fear and isolation. It helps focus our days and maintain wonder as we age. To be there is to be emotionally and spiritually in the present moment for your children, your spouse and yourself.[6]

What would it look like in your home for you to be fully present, in the moment, one on one with your child?

THE LOST ART OF BEING TOGETHER

It seems to me that we have a generation of families that have forgotten how to be together. Can we be together, without schedules, coaches, registration, tutors, enrichment or buying something?

When we love each other, we can relax with each other. We don't have to be entertained or amused. We don't have to be diverted from the uncomfortable reality that we are close—too close. We can appreciate what each family member brings to the gathering. We don't have to impress each other, show off, compete or get back at each other. We don't have to be afraid of each other, because mature love drives away fear.

I can be myself.

You can be yourself.

We can be family, together.

FOLLOW THE LEADER

As part of a family devotional time, a family I know had the children take turns leading in a brief game of Follow the Leader. Most kids love being in charge and watching their parents grimace as they take them through the paces. The Riveras have a daughter in high school and a son in middle school. The kids had a blast making their parents crawl under beds, through obstacle courses and up to places they would normally *never* go. The kids felt empowered by being the leaders. After the drill, all four collapsed with fatigue and laughter on the living-room floor.

"Dad got stuck a couple times. We weren't sure he would get out," the son reminisced gleefully.

"I wasn't sure either," said the dad.

"I think Dad and I are going to be sore tomorrow," admitted the mom.

"My stomach's sore from laughing," giggled the daughter.

It only took twenty minutes, at home, to build a fun memory.

Have we forgotten how to be together?

George Barna reminds us that love really does make a difference, and we should not leave our family's moral and spiritual development to others: "Each of us who has the privilege of relating to young children these days shares a special goal: *to help transform those children into spiritual champions. It will not happen by accident. . . .* We have no right to complain about how our children develop if we are not heavily and purposefully investing in those outcomes."[7]

Children who grow up in a home where the parents model this kind of dynamic love will most likely

- be relaxed and patient with family members
- feel valuable and connected with a strong sense of belonging

- find meaning in relationships, not possessions or fads
- have mentors who model the skills they need for life
- have the fortitude to challenge the antichild elements of our culture
- know how to persevere in relationships with unconditional love
- be receptive to correction and guidance
- feel free to be different and open to growth
- be grace oriented rather than performance oriented
- value unity and seek to foster a peaceful climate in the home

Stand–Up Kids in a Lie–Down World

Brooke called me with a request. "Dad, I have to write a paper for my comparative religion class. The topic is Christianity."

As a student at San Diego State University, she seldom called for help with her homework, but this project was strategic. "I know that Christ's resurrection sets Christianity apart from the other major religions. No other religious founder claimed to come alive after dying. I have to write a paper, and I might have to present it in class. It's full of crystal people, Buddhists, Muslims, partier-hedonists, and others like JWs and Mormons. What should I say? What is a credible resource?"

"Let me think—hey, don't you have *A Case for Christ* by Lee Strobel?"

"Yeah. That's the book that we used my last year of high school in my girls' small group. Oh yeah, I forgot about that. That's perfect. He writes from a journalist's point of view, so it doesn't sound too religious. Good idea. Thanks."

She wrote the paper and got a good grade on it; but more important, she learned to think. She learned to integrate the principles and teachings of her childhood and youth within an intellectually adversarial environment. She learned to challenge the other views expressed by the professor and her classmates. She learned to advocate a biblical worldview amid the din of postmodern confusion. She learned to be a warrior.

BOOT CAMP

As parents in the new millennium, we are preparing our kids for battle. We are training them to be courageous, capable and committed. We are modeling for them the virtues we want integrated into the fabric of their character. We want them to be influencers in a culture of passivity. We want stand-up kids in a lie-down world. To grow courageous kids, we need to see the home as a boot camp rather than a retreat.

Tim Kimmel says it well.

> The real test of a parenting model is how well equipped the children are to move into adulthood as vital members of the human race. Notice I didn't say "as vital members of the Christian community." We need to have kids that can be sent off to the most hostile universities, toil in the greediest work environments, and raise their families in the most hedonistic communities and yet not be the least bit intimidated by their surroundings.[1]

We have not done this well. We are better at the extremes, because they demand less of us. We either abandon our kids to the culture, figuring *kids will be kids,* or we isolate them in the Christian subculture, seeking to protect them from the "secular humanists" and other bogeymen out in "the world."

The problem with both the *give up* and the

We are preparing our kids for battle.

get out options is that neither is biblical. We really don't have either of these options for raising our kids, if we intend to be passionate followers of Christ. His marching orders are clear:

> Jesus came and told his disciples, "I have been given complete authority in heaven and on earth. Therefore, go and make disciples of all the nations, baptizing them in the name of the Father and the Son and the Holy Spirit. Teach these new disciples to obey all the commands I have given you. And be sure of this: I am with you always, even to the end of the age." (Matthew 28:18-20 NLT)

We aren't to blend in with the culture or hide from it; we are to influence it.

You may be familiar with this Scripture as Christ's Great Commission, but have you ever noticed what precedes it? "Some of the disciples still doubted Jesus." (verse 17). They were afraid. *What if this whole deal is a charade? Could it be some holy hoax? How can we withstand the evil forces that surround us? They killed Jesus. We will be next!*

Note that Jesus didn't say, "Isolate yourselves in the holy huddle." The Great Commission isn't "Go into your gate-guarded Christian cul-de-sac and hide out." It is "Go, and as you go, make disciples." We aren't to blend in with the culture or hide from it; we are to influence it.

Let's apply the Great Commission to parenting:

- We have been given the command to make God-followers of our children.

- We have been given authority by God to do this.

- We don't have to do it alone. We have the grace of the Father, the example of the Son and the indwelling power of the Holy Spirit to empower and guide us. We do it in the community of faith.

- The focus isn't protecting our kids; it's preparing them to be disciples and deliverers of God's good news in a way that fits the way he designed each of them.

- Priority is given to God's timeless commands and principles, not our petty rules, preferences or prejudices. This clarifies priorities and enhances the likelihood that our child will adopt Christlike qualities.

- God is with us at all times—even in the darkest hours. He won't abandon us.

- "To the end of the age": We really do have a limited time to prepare our kids and influence the culture. The clock is ticking, and we can see signs of the end.

I get tired of hearing about the "secularization" of our culture. It seems to me that we Christians have abandoned the culture to itself. The less we engage with the culture, the more it is left to its own devices; and the default setting of our society is secularization. The more we withdraw, the less influence we have on the lost world around us. We need to be *in the world, but not of it.*

SALT AND LIGHT

This book is about growing kids who can positively influence their world. It's about more than stopping "bad behavior"; it's about growing leaders for the next generation. It's about making disciples of our kids to affect the culture for the sake of Christ. It's about being and training our kids to be salt and light.

Jesus answers the cosmic question, *why are you here?* "Let me tell you why you are here. You're here to be salt-seasoning that brings out the God-flavors of this earth. If you lose your saltiness, how will people taste godliness? You've lost your usefulness and will end up in the garbage" (Matthew 5:13). He continues, "If I make you light-bearers, you don't think I'm going to hide you under a bucket, do you? I'm putting you on a light stand. Now that I've put you there on a hilltop, on a light stand—shine!" (Matthew 5:15-16 *The Message*).

> *Too many of us parents have been the bucket when we should have been the light stand.*

Too many of us parents have been the bucket when we should have been the light stand. We've been hiding the light, protecting the light, isolating the light, thinking that it is up to us to *keep* the light.

It isn't. It is up to us to *share* the light.

Are you a bucket or a light stand?

Mitali Perkins poses a strong challenge to equip our kids to engage popular culture:

> Instead of helplessly watching our kids take up permanent citizenship in popular culture, our job is to train them to influence it on behalf of the kingdom of God. Remember, we want them to be ambassadors, not immigrants. . . . The first step is to venture boldly and purposefully into popular culture with our kids in tow.[2]

FOUR WAYS TO SALT YOUR HOME

I like salty food. Pizza, chips, popcorn, pretzels and salted nuts parked in front of my TV with a game on, and I'm in hog heaven.

Salty food creates a thirst. Helping our kids adopt our values and learn crucial life skills is like feeding them salty food—we want to make our kids thirsty for what we have. The salt we offer is living out those values in front of them.

Virelle Kidder, mother of four grown children, puts it this way:

> "Let your conversation be always full of grace, seasoned with salt," Paul reminds us (Col. 4:6). Salt preserves goodness, adding flavor and interest to the otherwise commonplace elements of life. Salty parents who are full of grace and acceptance toward one another and their children create a thirst in their children for the things of God. They accomplish this in the simplest areas of everyday life.[3]

Kidder offers three ways to salt your home, and I've added a fourth.

1. *Show them you are real.* Faith and values are caught and taught. Give your kids multiple opportunities to see you applying the values you *said* were important. I call it "Tell 'n' Show."

   While writing the chapter on compassion, I took a break and went surfing with Brooke. Afterward, we went to our favorite burrito place. While we were standing outside waiting for our order, a homeless man approached me and asked me to buy him lunch. Just a few hours before, I had been studying 1 John 3:17: "But if one of you has enough money to live well, and sees a brother or sister in need and refuses to help—how can God's love be in that person?" (NLT).

We want to make our kids thirsty for what we have.

I knew what I had to do. All I had was a ten, so I handed it to him.

A toothless smile erupted. "God bless you, brother. My name is Billy." He offered his grimy hand.

"Nice to meet you, Billy." I shook his hand and smiled. "God bless *you*."

He got in line and ordered. I noticed all the other customers staring at us.

Our order came up, so I took it to the picnic table where Brooke was waiting. I wanted to wash my hands before I ate, but there wasn't any place to do so. Billy came over and sat down next to Brooke. He reeked of sweat, alcohol and urine. She wasn't too excited to have him inches away! We talked for a few minutes, heard a few crazy stories, then made an excuse to "finish the burritos in the truck." The stench was too overwhelming.

I've read somewhere that the best thing you can do for homeless people is smile at them—acknowledge that they are there. See them as a fellow human being, instead of looking away. All day they deal with people looking the other direction. So again I smiled at Billy and shook his hand as we said goodbye.

2. *Focus on character, not performance.* Ten years from now, what will you remember about raising your kids? Will it be the grade he got in English? The goal she scored in a soccer game? Or the few fleeting hours that his room was actually clean and picked up? Or will it be seeing your child mature over time to become responsible, caring and loving, with a heart for Christ and a commitment to change the world for him?

Will you remember the wacky fun times you shared? Having a ten-year window of perspective helps us not overreact to the annoyances of daily childrearing and helps us maintain a long-term perspective, hopefully with a sense of humor. When we focus on character, not performance, we are being salty parents; we are adding flavor to our home.

When we focus on character, not performance, we are being salty parents.

3. *Be available.* Salt doesn't do any good if it's not near the food. Can you imagine keeping table salt in the garage? Okay, you can use it to kill snails, but the main purpose is to add taste to food, and hopefully, you aren't eating your family dinners in the garage.

We need to be available to our kids. We need to make time to laugh, learn and live together. We need to learn how to be together.[4]

4. *Take risks.* Years ago Becky Pippert wrote an excellent book that helped me learn to take risks: *Out of the Salt Shaker and into the World.* It helped me become salt and light in my home and community. It helped me break out of the comfortable "bucket brigade" and discover the freedom, illumination and sense of mission up on the light stand. But it was risky. It was safer under the bucket. I might be knocked off the stand. The prevailing winds threaten to extinguish my light. The contrast between the light and the dark is greater on the stand than it was in the timid huddle of the bucket brigade where we shared a flickering glow.

But to become all that we are meant to be, to live up to our calling as children of the light, we have to throw off the bucket and perch ourselves on the light stand. This is how we make a difference. This is how we challenge the darkness.

So why don't we?

Giants in the Land

We are afraid of the giants in the land. God has given us the promised land, but there are giants here! There are enemies around us, and we are terrified of them. There are huge, intimidating enemies to contend with. We need to be brave and challenge them. We need to model courage for our kids as we challenge these formidable foes.

We have lost our preferred seating. We are in a post-Christian era. No longer does Christianity have the premier spot as the dominant worldview in North American culture. Because of secularization, Christianity has been relegated to the sidelines and is perceived as socially irrelevant and politically intrusive.

Faith and morality have become personal issues. "What you do in your private life isn't an issue." Privatization has swept our world, making individual fulfillment the new religion. The individual has become the politically correct idol of our times. "Pursue your own spirituality, but keep it private; don't drag your religion into the public forum or marketplace."

Most of us feel overwhelmed with too many choices—daunting and competing options that are continually thrust in our faces. We are forced to select from an astounding number of opinions, beliefs and ideologies, and many militantly oppose each other.

The other day I went out to a business lunch with a friend. The waitress brought us one of those stress-producing menus the size of an encyclopedia. I didn't even want to crack it open, so I asked my friend, "What are you having?"

"The chicken salad."

"I'll have the same." I didn't want to spend the mental energy looking at the sixty-four-page book.

If I can't handle lunch, how will I handle my family?

Another giant is the fuzziness of moral relativism: "What is true for you is not necessarily true for me." Morality is determined in the moment, not by some archaic absolute. Moral choices are "up to you." This giant makes it difficult to train and discipline your child: "Why should the parent determine what is right and wrong?"

As I said earlier, God has allowed these giants for our good. It's not absent-mindedness on his part. They are not here by mistake. They are here to challenge us, to help us grow, to keep our dependence on God, to keep us from being cocky.

KALEIDOSCOPE KIDS

Put all of these forces together, and you have a postmodern juggernaut. The challenge in parenting today's kids is discipling them toward definable absolutes in a world that does not believe in absolutes. If postmodernism can be defined as skepticism of any story that declares itself as *the* story, then the concept of a biblical worldview doesn't fit. No single view can speak for all people. We can't have a focused view, as through a telescope or a microscope, because that might leave somebody out. As a result, our kids have largely adopted the kaleidoscope as a metaphor for their worldview. They are children of the diversity-plurality-inclusiveness era.

> *We must disciple our children in definable absolutes in a world that does not believe in absolutes.*

As a result, they are confused. How can you get a clear picture of life through a kaleidoscope?

It's our job, as parents, to give them a clearer view.

THE BYSTANDER

James Emery White encourages us to step up to the plate.

> In the ancient world the influence of Christians acting as salt and
> light brought a stop to infanticide, ended slavery, liberated
> women and created hospitals, orphanages and schools. During
> the medieval era, Christianity kept classical culture alive through
> copying manuscripts, building libraries and inventing colleges
> and universities. In the modern era, Christians led the way in the
> development of science, political and economic freedom, and
> provided what is arguably the greatest source of inspiration for
> art, literature and music. What will Christians do in our day?
>
> The great danger is *nothing*.[5]

Ouch! That stings a little. But we *can* do something. We can influence our kids. I'd rather do that than build a library anyway. We just can't be bystanders and passively watch as our kids mix it up in the culture (don't forget the giants).

We need to be engaged. We need to take the initiative. We need to see our role as priests of the home. When you think about it, the only two institutions ordained by God are the church and the home. And in some ways, the home is a church. A child's first concepts of God are likely to be forged at home. It is the first place children learn community. The home is the child's first experience with others.

Family life is first of all a life.

As Thomas Merton said, "The spiritual life is first of all a *life*."[6] Being spiritual isn't just talking or meditating or lighting candles, it's living. Family life, too, is first of all a *life*. It is living out what we believe to be true in front of our kids. Our values, our convictions, the things that we say we'd die for—expressed amid the brushing of teeth, the paying of bills, the carting of kids around in the minivan, and the welcome relief of the pillow as our weary head descends for the night.

Dear parent, what you do matters. The temptation of our era is to falsely believe we can't do anything. *The giants are too big. Our children are lost to the culture.*

The hazard is assuming that things do not depend on us, that we don't have any influence on our children. But what we do with our children does matter. We can influence our world, one child at a time.

> *We can influence our world, one child at a time.*

THE GAME

My early twenties friend Josh Weidmann provides some wise musings in his book *Dad, If You Only Knew:*

> After my dad graduated from the Academy, he stayed on as football coach before heading off to flight school. He said one of the most interesting things about coaching was that you spend about ten hours on the practice field each week for each four-hour game. Most of the practice time is spent running plays against an opponent's different formations. When game time came, players had already experienced an opponent's move. Dad says parenting is like this. The home is the practice field. Dad, the coach, is there watching, listening, directing, encouraging, and correcting. During game time, coaches stand on the sidelines providing input only when players come off the field. My dad says "the game" is when teens leave and go to college,

get a job, get married, or move away. Then, young adults will be forced to apply what parents have taught. They may also discover what wasn't taught.[7]

Are you preparing your kids to be in the game? Have you run opposing formations so they will be ready? Do you know the sneaky strategies of your opponents? Have you watched video footage of their play so your child will be equipped? Have you carefully paid attention to your own child's strengths and weaknesses, and do you have a game plan to maximize her assets and minimize her liabilities?

Will your child be ready for the game?

TRAVIS'S TRANSFORMATION

Our friends invited us to their church's Christmas musical. During the intermission, while we sipped hot cider and cocoa, a young man came up to me, "Hey Tim, I thought that was you! Merry Christmas!"

His sparkling eyes and broad smile projected excitement and contentment. His full head of brown curly hair and stylish clothes reminded me of models I've seen in surf magazines.

"Ah, yeah . . . good to see you too." My hand met his, "How are you doing?"

"Very well. Things are much better. Gee, it's good to see you. Howz it with you?"

I stared at his face before I responded. *Who is this kid?* He looked vaguely familiar, but I didn't know where from. Finally I stammered, "Ah, it's going well. I'm enjoying my writing and speaking."

"And your coaching practice?"

"Going alright, thanks. So what are you up to? Do you go to this church?"

"Yeah, I've been going here for years. Well . . ." an expansive smile emerged as he paused for emphasis, "I'm at a Christian college, have a part-time job and am helping out at church with the middle school ministry. And things are a hundred percent better at home."

I was still baffled. *Where do I know him from?*

As my brain whirled at half a megahertz, a friendly-looking woman walked up and smiled at me.

"Remember my mom?"

I did. And now it started to come back. "Wow, it's good to see you, and I barely recognize your son!"

"Yes, it's remarkable. We are really pleased with the changes in Travis's life."

That's right! His name is Travis.

"Did he tell you about college?" Her eyes danced as she flashed a smile.

"Yes, he did. That's great!"

"It's been eighteen months since we brought him to see you, and by God's grace, we are in a completely different place. Thanks for your help." She gave me a hug, and then left us to talk.

"I'm reading one of your books at school. It's one on nurturing the soul of the youth worker. I want to be a youth minister."

"That's awesome, Travis. You'll make an amazing youth pastor!"

"Thanks. Good to see you." He grabbed my hand and left.

Eighteen months prior he was an unmotivated, high school partier with total disregard for his mother's rules and values. He was failing at school and she was about to ship him off to "brat camp."

What had made the difference?

His mom had moved from protection to preparation. For years she had tried to control his behavior. When he didn't live up to her expectations, she criticized and belittled him.

I coached him to prepare for life as an independent young man.

"You are sixteen now. In less than two years you will be eighteen and you could be on your own. Let's work on preparing you for life. Are you ready for this?"

"Will it get my mom off my back?"

"That's the plan."

"Well, alright. Let's do it."

The following is a summary of what I went over with Travis and his mom:

We all make mistakes, but we need to live in "no matter what" homes. These are homes where kids are allowed to be kids and parents don't have to be perfect and nobody will be written off—*no matter what.* Grace is always in residence.

Our words powerfully shape our relationships and the future of our child. Declare positive words of life over kids like Travis rather than condemning predictions of doom and failure. Speak loving words of approval and encouragement to your child.

The risk is worth it. When we move from fear-based parenting of "keep them safe" to a "prepare them for life" approach, it is scary. We can't control all of the variables, but for kids twelve years and up, it's the more effective approach because the parent shares a common goal with the child. Some parents try teaching their kids values like training them to swim on the linoleum in the kitchen. They don't want to risk real water because they might drown.[8]

Raising nice kids is not enough; we want to raise courageous kids with character. Safe and protected kids tend to be wimpy and spoiled. When our emphasis is on growing courageous champions, they become wise and discerning, making them actually safer.

Preparing your child to change his world means focusing on his heart more than his behavior, looks or accomplishments. I'm discovering that if we get our child's heart right, we don't get sidetracked by the externals. Travis's mom was so worried about his grades and appearance that it drove a wedge between them. When she learned to focus on the internals, their relationship improved and Travis assumed responsibility for his grades, but she had to sacrifice these first.

You are not alone. Raising stand-up kids in a lie-down world requires God's power. A faith-based, grace-oriented approach to parenting affirms the unique personalities of our children, and is alert to the corrosive cultural elements, but is focused on confidence in God rather than the worries of the world. That is why our influence as parents and grandparents rests primarily on our personal relationship with God. Sure, there are enemies in the land. But we do not have to be afraid.

> He who fears the LORD has a secure fortress,
>   and for his children it will be a refuge. (Proverbs 14:26 NIV)

We don't need to be afraid of the culture for our children. We simply need awe and respect for God. He is our fortress. He is a refuge for our kids. With his strength, they can change their world.

Appendix 1

Our Family's Core Values and Mission

YOUR CORE VALUES

What are the most important values in your family? Do your kids know these are critical? Do both parents agree on the ranking of values? This worksheet will help you develop and communicate your top values.

A "value" is an ideal that is desirable. It is a quality that we want to model in our own lives and see developed in the lives of our kids. For instance, honesty is a very important value, for without it you can't have trust in your relationships.

Take time in writing your answers to the following questions.

1. When time and energy are in short supply, what should we make sure we cover in parenting our children? List a few ideas. Then circle the nonnegotiables.

2. What are the "we'd like to get around to these" values? These are the semi-negotiables.

3. What were the top three values of each of your families of origin (the family you grew up in)?

Father	Mother
1.	1.
2.	2.
3.	3.

4. Think about a healthy, positive family—one that serves as a role model for you. What would you say are their top three values?
   1.
   2.
   3.

5. What are three or four favorite Scripture verses that communicate elements of a healthy family?
   1.
   2.
   3.
   4.

   Based on these verses, what are the three or four principles from Scripture that you'd like to see evidenced in your family?
   1.
   2.
   3.
   4.

6. What values are your "pound the table with passion" values? What are the ones that you feel very strongly about? (You may already have them listed.) To help you with this, complete the following sentences:

More families need to . . .

The problem with today's families is . . .

DEVELOPING YOUR FAMILY'S MISSION STATEMENT

Besides writing out your core values, you will do well to develop a family mission statement (or covenant). These important documents will shape your family. The founders of the United States knew that guiding documents would keep us on course as a fledgling democracy; so too will these documents guide your family as you seek to be purposeful.

Sample mission statement:

We exist to love each other and advance God's timeless principles and his kingdom on earth.

Complete the following:

1. Our family exists to . . .

2. What are some activities or behaviors that you imagine your family carrying out?

3. Describe some qualities of character that you can envision your family being known for.

4. What is unique about your family? What makes you different? What are you known for? What sets you apart?

5. What do you hope to do with and through your family that will outlive you? What noble cause greater than yourselves do you want your family to pursue?

6. With these five questions completed, look for a Scripture that supports the basic ideas of your rough-draft concepts for your family mission statement. If there are several candidates, talk about them thoughtfully and choose one, writing it out here:

7. Using the sample as a template, your five questions and your family Scripture, write a rough draft of your family mission statement:

8. Rewrite the mission statement, keeping the same concepts but changing the order of the mission statement. This is simply to give you two options.

9. Discuss this mission statement as a family if the kids are old enough. Discuss it with a few other friends or extended family members. Any feedback?

10. Pray about your family mission statement for a couple of weeks, asking God to affirm it or help you edit it. Then write up the final version. Consider making a permanent version of your family mission statement to hang on a wall in your home.

Appendix 2
Target at 18

What We Want Our Child to Be at 18

Spiritual   To have a growing and vibrant faith in Christ

To be able to explain and defend their faith

To be in community with other believers the same age

Social   To be able to make wise decisions about friends and activities

To be able to relate to a wide variety of people in diverse situations

Physical   To be in good health and maintain habits of an active lifestyle

To preserve their virginity until they are married

To live a substance-abuse-free lifestyle

Emotional   To feel capable, confident of self and of God-given abilities

To draw boundaries (not be taken advantage of by others—personal courage)

Mental   To be prepared for opportunities encountered in the future

To be lifelong learners and perform up to their potential academically

To think critically and biblically with a Christian worldview

Character   To be honest, fair, authentic, dependable, forgiving, compassionate, generous, courageous and loving

To listen well

To have vision

Life Skills To develop skills in finances: know how to maintain a checking account, balance the account, pay bills and maintain a personal budget

To have a sense of personal purpose: know strengths, weaknesses, talents, passion and have a sense of God's destiny, design and duty for their life

To make college or vocational school decision by eighteenth birthday

To have experience in serving others and in ministry

To know how to plan nutritious meals, shop for groceries, cook and maintain a home (laundry, care for clothes, etc.)

To know how to drive, purchase auto insurance, maintain a car and deal with driving challenges (weather, accidents, breakdowns, etc.)

To master basics of personal organization (scheduling, records, storage)

TARGET WORKSHEET

To begin developing your own aims for your child, jot down some of your ideas in the following categories.

What are the most important components of the four qualities and skill areas my children need to begin life on their own?

1. To make wise decisions:

2. To possess character:

3. To have vision and purpose:

4. To have and use life skills:

Appendix 3

Countdown to Independence

HELP YOUR KIDS DO MORE AS YOU DO LESS

At each birthday or every six months, record milestones that you'd like to see in terms of freedom and responsibility for your child. You will need to make accommodations for each child; some may be delayed, while others may be advanced. Be flexible, keeping in mind the goal is not following a prescribed formula, but a general process of helping your child do more as you do less.

Example: at 5 years old – Learn to dress myself

8 years old – Make my own sack lunch.

10 years old – Go to summer camp.

12 years old – Get to choose my own back-to-school clothes.

14 years old – Make dinner for my family once a week. Get to stay up until eleven on weekends.

On the next page is a chart you can use to plan your child's "Countdown to Independence."

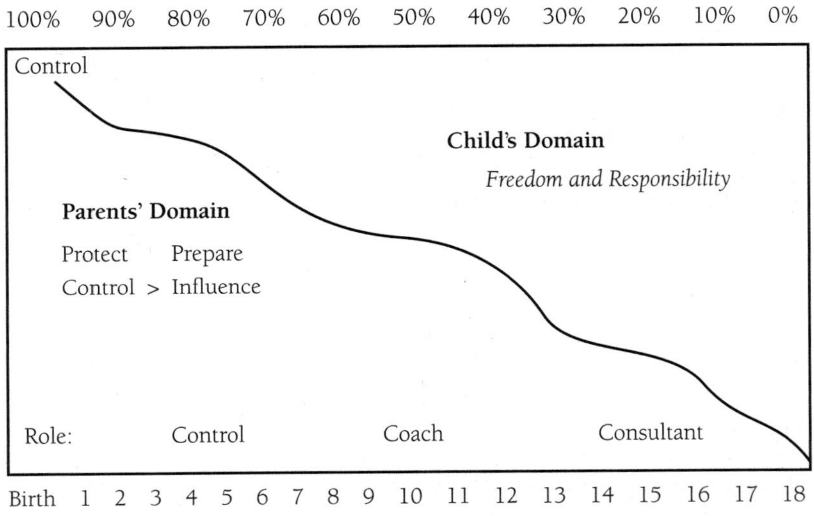

Birth to age 6 ______________________________

Age 7 to 12 ______________________________

Age 13 to 18 ______________________________

Figure 1. Countdown to independence

Appendix 4

Consequences Worksheets

DEVELOPING CONSEQUENCES

1. Define your expectations in writing:
   a. I expect my child to . . .

   b. This is important to me because it is a way of expressing the value of . . .

   c. The positive consequence for the child living up to the expectations is . . .

   d. The negative consequence for the child *not* living up to the expectations is . . .

2. Inform your child of the value, behavior (rule) and consequences (both positive and negative).

3. Remind your child that it is *their* choice. You job is to enforce the agreement, but the choice is up to the child (moral responsibility).

4. Refer to the agreement and reinforce it as necessary.

GUIDELINES FOR USING CONSEQUENCES

Less is better. Keep consequences as minimal as possible.

Short-term. Keep consequences as immediate as possible.

Realistic. Keep consequences reasonable and enforceable.

Correspondence. Correspond the consequence to the misbehavior.

Connection. Connect the value you are seeking to teach with the rule and preferred behavior and the consequence. Emphasize the positive value more than the negative behavior.

For each year through age eighteen, this table suggests for your consideration a value or virtue that is age appropriate, a corresponding rule, and a positive and negative consequence.

CONSEQUENCE PLANNER

Age of Child	Value/Virtue	Behavior/Rule	Consequence Positive	Consequence Negative
1-2	Consideration	Make requests with normal voice; don't scream	Parent will consider request	Timeout and request not considered
2-3	Kindness	Learn to share	Will be able to use toys	Loss of toy not shared for one day
3-4	Help others	Do one thing each day to help Mommy	Will get to do big-kid tasks like set the table	Loss of privilege (e.g., TV or videos)
4-5	Responsible use of one's possessions	Put away toys; don't lose things	Will be able to use school supplies	Loss of crayons and scissors for two days
6-7	Honesty	Tell the truth	Trusted to play at friend's house	Can't play at friend's house
7-8	Fairness	Make sure things are "even"	Enjoy playing games and with friends	Loss of a game or friend time
8-9	Obedience	Listen carefully and follow instructions/ rules	Can choose how to spend free time	Loss of free time = timeout
9-10	Self-control	Get up on time and get ready for school	Can stay up till 8:30 p.m.	Must go to bed at 7:30 p.m.
11-12	Decision making	Make wise choices with time and friends	Freedom to make choices	Loss of some of these choices
13-14	Responsibility	Weekly clean room and do laundry (due Friday, 6:00 p.m.)	Go out Friday night	Can't go out Friday night
15	Courage	Develop/write personal standards regarding drinking, dating and drugs	Enjoy time with friends (unsupervised)	Loss of free time, or time with friends will be supervised
16	Discernment	Alert to dangers in people and on the road	Gets to drive	Loss of driving
17	Compassion	Other-centered, not self-centered	Choice of weekend activities	Must spend Saturday serving others
18	Independence	Self-reliant; contributes money to pay expenses	Enjoy freedom and parents' financial support	Loss of parents' financial support

Notes

Chapter 1: More Than *Nice*

[1]Adapted from Henri J. M. Nouwen, *The Genesee Diary* (New York: Doubleday, 1981), pp. 178-79.

[2]Anna Quindlen, "The Good Enough Mother," *Newsweek,* February 21, 2005, p. 50.

[3]Jeffrey M. Jones, "Parents of Young Children Are Most Stressed Americans," Gallup News Service, Poll Analyses, November 8, 2002.

[4]Judith Warner, "Mommy Madness," *Newsweek*, February 21, 2005, p. 45.

[5]Adapted from David Elkind, *The Hurried Child: Growing Up Too Fast Too Soon* (Reading, Mass.: Addison-Wesley, 1985), pp. 28-29, emphasis added.

[6]Adapted from Robert Shaw, *The Epidemic: The Rot of American Culture, Absentee and Permissive Parenting, and the Resultant Plague of Joyless, Selfish Children* (New York: HarperCollins, 2003), pp. 4-5.

Chapter 2: Parenting as Discipleship

[1]Tim Stafford, *Never Mind the Joneses: Building Core Christian Values in a Way That Fits Your Family* (Downers Grove, Ill.: InterVarsity Press, 2004), p. 21.

[2]Bruno Bettelheim, *A Good Enough Parent* (New York: Alfred A. Knopf, 1987), p. 99.

[3]George Barna, *Transforming Children into Spiritual Champions* (Ventura, Calif.: Regal, 2003), p. 48.

[4]Timothy Smith, *The Seven Cries of Today's Teens: Hear Their Hearts, Make the Connection* (Nashville: Integrity, 2003), p. 167.

[5]George Gallup Jr., "What Americans Believe About Fatherhood and the Role of Religion," in *The Faith Factor in Fatherhood: Renewing the Sacred Vocation of Fathering,* ed. Don E. Eberly (Lanham, Md.: Rowman & Littlefield, 2002), p. 55.

Chapter 3: Clarifying Vision

[1]Gordon MacDonald, *The Effective Father* (Wheaton, Ill.: Tyndale House, 1977), p. 183-84.

[2]George Barna, "Parents Describe How They Raise Their Children," *The Barna Update,* February 28, 2005, p. 1; available at www.barna.org.

[3]Doug Colligan, "Happiness: How to Have It Now," *Reader's Digest*, March 2005, p. 94.

[4]Barna, "Parents Describe," p. 3, emphasis added.

[5]Tim Kimmel, *Raising Kids Who Turn Out Right* (Sisters, Ore.: Multnomah Press, 1993), p. 14.

[6]U.S. Census Bureau home page, March 30, 2001: <www.census.gov>.

Chapter 4: Embracing Authenticity

[1]Tim Kimmel, *Grace Based Parenting: Set Your Family Free* (Nashville: Thomas Nelson, 2004), p. 14.

[2]Ibid., p. 21.

Chapter 5: Learning to Listen

[1]Michael Medved and Diane Medved, *Saving Childhood: Protecting Our Children from the National Assault on Innocence* (New York: HarperPerennial, 1999), 178.

[2]Timothy Smith, *The Seven Cries of Today's Teens: Hear Their Hearts, Make the Connection* (Nashville: Integrity, 2003), p. 118.

[3]Ibid., p. 136.

[4]Michael P. Nichols, *The Lost Art of Listening: How Learning to Listen Can Improve Relationships* (New York: Guilford, 1995), pp. 197-98.

[5]H. Norman Wright and Gary Oliver, *Raising Kids to Love Jesus* (Ventura, Calif.: Regal, 1999), p. 64.

Chapter 6: Showing Empathy

[1]Donald Miller, *Blue Like Jazz* (Nashville: Thomas Nelson, 2003), p. 105.

[2]Robert Shaw, *The Epidemic* (New York: HarperCollins, 2003), pp. 106-7.

[3]Paul D. Hastings, Carolyn Zahn-Waxler, National Institutes of Mental Health and University of Colorado, Boulder, research summary, reported in ibid., p. 146.

[4]William J. Doherty, *Take Back Your Kids* (Notre Dame, Ind.: Sorin, 2002), pp. 15-16.

Chapter 7: Demonstrating Compassion

[1]Historical details adapted from <www.soon.org.uk/true_stories/holocaust.htm>.

[2]Douglas K. Huneke, *The Moses of Rovno* (Tiburon, Calif.: Compassion House, 1985), pp. 178-84.

[3]Jan Johnson, *Growing Compassionate Kids: Helping Kids See Beyond Their Backyard* (Nashville: Upper Room, 2001), p. 23.

[4]Ibid., pp. 26-27.

Chapter 8: Developing Discernment

[1]G. Richard Louv, *Childhood's Future* (Boston: Houghton Mifflin, 1990), p. 19.

[2]George Barna, *Transforming Children into Spiritual Champions* (Ventura, Calif.: Regal/Gospel Light, 2003), p. 51.

[3]Tim Kimmel, *Why Christian Kids Rebel* (Nashville: W Publishing Group, 2004), p. 183.

[4]Barna, *Transforming Children,* pp. 77-78.

Chapter 9: Courageously Setting Boundaries

[1]Henry Cloud and John Townsend, *Boundaries* (Grand Rapids: Zondervan, 1992), p. 29.

[2]Ibid., p. 131.

Chapter 10: Choosing Contentment

[1]"Rich Parents Seek to Instill Values: Many Worry Children Won't Have Work Ethic," *Ventura County Star,* June 13, 2005, p. A1.

[2]Tim Stafford, *Never Mind the Joneses: Building Core Christian Values in a Way That Fits Your Family* (Downers Grove, Ill.: InterVarsity Press, 2004), p. 177.

[3]Phil McGraw, *Family First* (New York: Simon & Schuster, 2004), p. 176.

[4]Tim Kimmel, *Grace-Based Parenting: Set Your Family Free* (Nashville: Thomas Nelson, 2004), pp. 142-43.

[5]Hugh Hewitt, *In, but Not Of* (Nashville: Thomas Nelson, 2003), p. 6.

[6]Stafford, *Never Mind the Joneses,* p. 191.

Chapter 11: Loving Passionately

[1]Timothy Smith, *The Seven Cries of Today's Teens: Hear Their Hearts, Make the Connection* (Nashville: Integrity, 2003), p. 167.

[2]Chap Clark, *Hurt: Inside the World of Today's Teenagers* (Grand Rapids: Baker Academic, 2004), pp. 42-43.

[3]George Gallup Jr., "What Americans Believe About Fatherhood and the Role of Religion," in *The Faith Factor in Fatherhood: Renewing the Sacred Vocation of Fathering,* ed. Don E. Eberly (Lanham, Md.: Rowman & Littlefield,) p. 55, emphasis added.

[4]David Popenoe, *Life Without Father* (New York: Free Press, 1996), p. 191.

[5]Tim Kimmel, *Why Christian Kids Rebel* (Nashville: W Publishing Group, 2004), pp. 186-87.

[6]John Trent, *Be There! Making Deep, Lasting Connections in a Disconnected World*

(Colorado Springs: Waterbrook, 2000), p. 5.

[7]George Barna, *Transforming Children into Spiritual Champions* (Ventura, Calif.: Regal/ Gospel Light, 2003), p. 136, emphasis adapted.

Chapter 12: Stand-Up Kids in a Lie-Down World

[1]Tim Kimmel, *Grace-Based Parenting: Set Your Family Free* (Nashville: Thomas Nelson, 2004), pp. 9.

[2]Mitali Perkins, *Ambassador Families: Equipping Your Kids to Engage Popular Culture* (Grand Rapids: Brazos, 2005), p. 24.

[3]Virelle Kidder, *Loving, Launching and Letting Go* (Nashville: Broadman & Holman, 1995), p. 75.

[4]Ibid., pp. 75-80.

[5]James Emery White, *Serious Times: Making Your Life Matter in an Urgent Day* (Downers Grove, Ill.: InterVarsity Press, 2004), p. 154.

[6]Thomas Merton, *Thoughts in Solitude* (New York: Farrar, Straus & Giroux, 1958), p. 56.

[7]Adapted from Josh Weidmann and James Weidmann, *Dad, If You Only Knew: Eight Things Teens Want to Tell Their Fathers (But Don't)* (Sisters, Ore.: Multnomah Publishers, 2005), p. 127.

[8]Adapted from Kimmel, *Grace-Based Parenting,* p. 120.